# THE COMPETENT YOUTH

*I am competent & fit to run; and I was.
Also to encourage the Youths across Africa to
advocate and participate in good governance.*

By

## JAMES USEGHAN

# The Competent Youth



James Useghan

@jamesuseghan

@jamesuseghan

jayuseghan@yahoo.com

www.jamesuseghan.com

08057390306, 07068976892

First Print: 2020

ISBN: **978-978-983-906-3**



Printed by:
**Egghead Colours**
Tel: 08023908591
E-mail: akes_designs@yahoo.com

# TABLE OF CONTENTS

# DEDICATION

This book is dedicated to my immediate late younger sister, Christiana Ebimiyen, who stood by me all through the election period; and to the youths in the struggle for good governance in Africa. I trust that with total commitment and focused mindset to liberate ourselves from the shackles of economic and political bondage, we will surely get the good governance that we truly seek and richly.

# ACKNOWLEDGEMENT

All thanks be to God Almighty for the new lease of life given to me to continue on this journey and bringing this book to reality. I express my deep sense of gratitude to my loving wife, Mrs. Oluwabunmi James Useghan, who has ever been brainstorming, supportive, tolerating and encouraging me in developing this book from the beginning.

I appreciate my Parents in-law, Comrade and Mrs. Samuel Akindele, for allowing me have her as my wife. My sincere gratitude goes to my father in the Lord and his wife, Rev Dr. and Rev. (Mrs.) Benson Omomukuyo, for always encouraging me to be the best I can in my activities in God's vineyard. Thank you so much for helping me through this book and adjusting where necessary.

My sincere gratitude goes to P.A. Shonekan, whom God used to make me contest the Senatorial race in Ondo South. We will surely fulfill destiny by His Grace.

I must not fail to acknowledge my parents, Mr. and Mrs.

Oluwanishola Useghan, for their counsel and prayers all through my life. Your wonderful closeness has brought a lot of meaning to my life. It will be an unpardonable omission if I fail to recognize Mr. Ken Edward Etete, my boss, mentor and inspiration to my doggedness in life to solving problems, enabling people and creating value here on earth.

To my other mentor, Dr. Chris Ekiyor, who inspired me in advocacy and activism, I will always appreciate that humble beginning. You gave birth to a lion (me).

Super Comrade Evah, thank you: for your timely contribution to the publication of this book.

Special appreciation to Ayanniyi  Taiwo and Michael Ogunsina that helped me through the development of this piece. It was a wonderful exploration through our  late nights discussing the better ways to have this book.

To my editor Ambassador Omololu Olubakinde, thank you very much for putting your eagle- eye into this book to suit every reader.

To Century Group and Christ Anointed Kingdom Int'l Church, you have been amazing to my life's journey. First Massive Literati (FML), and to every youth that is inspired by this book, thank you for always advocating for a just and egalitarian society.

Our desires will not be cut short. (Aluta Continua!!!)

# FOREWORD

The Nigerian youths are an endangered generation when it comes to political participation and representation in Nigeria. They have, at various times, been degraded, devalued and unappreciated. They have been variously tagged and labelled, albeit uncharitably, lazy, immature, unprepared, unserious and unfit to rule the country at the top echelon of governance. Consequently, they have been unjustifiably sidelined and denied political space, place and grace to serve their fatherland. The political system in operation in Nigeria puts much emphasis on money power to access political power. It has conspired with the elite class of very old and recycled politicians to deny the youths the opportunity to attain political leadership of this country.

**The Competent Youth-** written by Brother (Senatorial candidate) James Useghan, is an autobiography of an upstart who rose from poverty and obscurity to national prominence and significance through the dint of hard work and God's grace. The book, among other things, advert attention to the unfortunate and the indefensible neglect of the Nigerian youths in the political affairs of the country.

The seven-chapter book can be described as an odyssey of a young man, who was born in poverty, raised in poverty, lived among poverty-stricken people, in a depraved environment, with a very slim chance of surviving his harsh birth circumstances. But, against all odds, he did not only survive those hardships, he went on to record notable achievements, as a result of strong determination, will power and abundance of God's grace that he enjoyed. This young man did not allow the poverty of his family control his future, nor allow it to determine his destiny. He fought all odds, including the threat of premature death, and, has of today, succeeded in attaining his present level of socio-political relevance in the country.

Every chapter of this book gives the reader a different insight and deeper perspective of the author's personality and bio-physiological compositions. They go on to reveal the diverse talents and gifts that the author has been generously endowed with by God. He is a young man of many parts, who can be described as a 'Jack of all trades but master of all'. He has vast experience in many areas of human endeavours.

In his struggle to survive and overcome different challenges of life, he tried his hands on many things. At different times in his life, he was involved in the following professions: music, singing, song writing and composition, acting, comedy, teaching, bus conducting, event planning and workshop organizing and religion. Today he also is an inventor, an author and a politician. What a competent youth!

The publication of the book, **The Competent Youth**, is timely and a welcome development. Three major issues are highlighted and addressed in the book. The Author brings into focal perspective and national consciousness the plight, suffering and the neglect of the people of the Niger Delta where he comes from. The book depicts a cruel irony of life in which a region that is endowed with so much oil resources but has its people live in squalor, abject poverty and deprivation; lacking in essential things of life. The author feels strongly concerned about the plight of his people in the Niger Delta. He believes the region deserves better treatment and more attention. He wants competent, passionate, committed and selfless young and dynamic people to represent the region at the National Assembly as a way of bringing fast economic development to that region.

In addressing the problem of the poor-participation of the Nigerian youths in political processes and leadership, he counsels that the youths should develop skills in different areas of human endeavours and stir up their spirit for political participation, while developing clear vision, workable ideology and having godly wisdom in their preparation for public service. Additionally, the author suggests an amendment to the electoral law of 'Not Too Young To Run' to include 'Not Too Poor To Run'. He explains that without such an amendment, most Nigerian youths would still be unable to contest and win elections at the highest level of governance because of the oppressive financial requirements for nomination and participation.

The third major area of focus of the book has to do with the level of corruption in the electioneering process in the country. The book observes that the process has been seriously corrupted and compromised through monetization of political participation. The book calls the process 'Transactional politics, where 'money' is the language of communication, while politics is being seen as a business and investment venture; not an avenue to serve the people.

The author recommends **Transformational** politics in place of **Transactional** politics in which selfless service, egalitarian ideology and national patriotism would be the motivating factors for those seeking political offices. It would no longer be business as usual but business for the rapid transformation of the national economy, through correct political participation for the betterment of the people of the country.

I believe strongly that **The Competent Youth** is a *must read book* for every youth who is aspiring to succeed in life and who wants to leave his marks on the sands of time. As young as the author is, he has paid the necessary due to get to where he is today. He has demonstrated uncanny ability in confronting and overcoming those daunting challenges that should have stopped him from fulfilling his destiny in life. His faith in God and the servant of God is legendary. Even at the threat of death, he still insisted that he should be taken to his church for prayer by his General Overseer, instead of being taken straight to the hospital. His readiness to accept challenges and confront them headlong is amazing and commendable personal attribute. The author never stopped putting and deploring all his resources and efforts into any venture he believed in. This is one of the reasons for his success in life.

His numerous achievements in life; his hunger to succeed; and his indefatigable ability to overcome, are a great lesson for every youth to emulate. Those achievements belie his age and his physical frame, thus confirming the popular saying that *"the wisdom of Solomon has nothing to do with the age of Methuselah or that a hood does not make a Monk!*

It is very easy to observe and see in the book, **The Competent Youth**, impatience, anger and frustration in the language of the author, while discussing the neglect of Niger Delta Region and the impoverishment of its people, including the Nigerian Youths dilemma in political leadership and the endemic corruption that has bedevilled Nigerian political system. One can perceive nationalistic tendencies in his spirit and also activism and militancy in his attitude. I can say, without mincing words, that the James I know carries the fire of militancy in his bones and the flames of nationalism in his heart. He is Marcus Garvey, Martin Luther King Jr, Kwame Nkrumah, Nnamdi Azikwe and Obafemi Awolowo, all wrapped up together in that little frame of his. I see him exploding into something great and big in the near future. Look out for him!

Before that happens, please get yourself a copy of the book: **The Competent Youth** in preparation for what is to come. You will be glad you did.

God bless.

**Revd. Dr. Benson I. Omomukuyo**
*Christ Anointed Kingdom Int'l Church*
*Lagos.*
*May 18, 2020*

# INTRODUCTION

Raising the question of competency in Africa leadership will assuredly generate a wide range of opinions and extensive arguments, most especially in politics. The African nations, for decades, have suffered in the hands of leaders (authoritarians, monarchy and democratically elected officials) that have fallen short of what could be considered as ecumenical metrics of competence. There have been megalomaniac leaders who only cling to power for the luxury and extravagance accruables, without ever considering the effects of such addiction on the sustainability of the nations.

One can begin to wonder the rationale behind Africans' unquenchable thirst for power, whereas only very little have changed as a direct effect of good leadership in the continent. Could it have been that many of these leaders were (and still are) blinded by egocentric motives or the ignoble appetite for power to oppress and lead ostensibly opulent and affluent life?

The need for democratic transition of power has resulted into massive riots, popular protests and civil wars in countries like Senegal, Burundi, Democratic Republic of Congo, Equatorial Guinea, and Zimbabwe, among others. It is a great concern that calls for sober reflection.

A more peculiar revelation of the unnecessary clinging to power of African leaders was offered by the recently ousted octogenarian President Abdelaziz Bouteflika of Algeria who, after two decades of authoritarian rulership, decided to cling to power even when his body was frail and ailed. Nigeria is not excluded from this leadership travail cum impasse on the African soil. The nation has been governed by leaders who lack the required philosophy and pragmatism to make a significant change, yet most of these leaders are tempted to hold to power forever by amending the constitution in their favour or in furtherance of their megalomaniac scheme.

More unfortunately is the fact that as the people strives fiercely and fanatically every four years to proffer lasting solution to the prevailing leadership problem of the nation, the process seems to be in cycles. The problem appears to be worse at every turn than the previous. This now raises a salient question of whether we are progressing or retrogressing as a country or perhaps that we have been looking at the wrong direction, and the solution lies unknowingly elsewhere?.

Distilled to the fundamental, the underlying consequences of these cyclic unproductive processes are felt tremendously across board and deeply entrenched in the economic stagnancy, democratic retrogression, and technological setback of African nations. The recent discourses to dissect the fundamentals of the pressing problems have centred on the questions of competences and capability of public servants. Strident voices, primarily from the younger generation, have risen to challenge the competences and effectiveness of these leaders, who are predominantly geriatrics.

These problems have raised striking concerns for all and sundry, most especially the young generation, who now believe that they need to take the bull by the horns and shape the direction of their country to afford them the prosperity they deserve.

The 'Not-Too-Young To Run bill' recently signed into law by the current administration is an inevitable answer to the popular outcry of the youths, for their value to be priced higher and ultimately included in government. There has been constitutionally entrenched limiting bar which excluded the legally recognized age range of youths from holding strategic political and public offices.

The 'Not-Too-Young To Run bill' lowers this bar considerably to accommodate active participations of youths in politics. This writer also maximizes the opportunity afforded by this constitution amendment to contest in the last general elections in the country. The process, experience and outcome of the elections are documented extensively in further pages of this book. They, in fact, necessitated this book.

Not to allow ourselves to be pulled by the nose and ruled by the surge of emotions, we should ask ourselves whether competence and capability as requested by popular opinion for effective public service are a function of youthfulness or senescence Or, perhaps, the agitation for youth inclusiveness in governance was another stratagem by the enemies of the nation to reincarnate through their stooges to further their destructive ventures by proxy If not, then we must critically examine the quality of leaders we desire and ensure our youths are adequately prepared and equipped to measure up to the standard.

Now that youths have been constitutionally invited to actively participate and contribute their sacred and patriotic quota in public leadership, it will be a grievous sin and disservice to the nation to trivialize the question of competency and capability. We must call a solemn assembly for our youths and stir in them a zealous and patriotic passion to seek to better them through acquisition of profound knowledge, requisite skills, immaculate insights and panoramic wisdom in preparation for public service.

This book is a reflection of the expectation of Nigeria on her youths. On the foregoing pages of this book are chronicled the story of my life, how I beat the odds to embrace self-development (still doing so), and to weather through the mountains of disadvantages mobilized by my immediate society. I also highlight my leadership experiences from childhood, teenage and adulthood. Also recorded was the health struggle that almost took my life in December, 2010. Most importantly, the book also extensively narrates my experience as a senatorial candidate in the last general elections. The book concludes with a call to the youths to rise above their limitations and take responsibility for their future.

Permit me to authoritatively assert that this book

encompasses all that it takes to prepare a competent youth that will proactively cause the needed transformation in our national landscape.

Our problems are deeply entrenched and we need more youths to tackle them head-on. I can assure you, by virtue of the practicality of my experience, that the best days are ahead of us and we can optimize them productively if only we consciously take up the responsibility to acquire the requisite skills and competence to initiate the positive change.

The intention of this book is, not to malign, misjudge or mispresent facts for selfish aggrandizement or to earn cheap popularity. The narratives are presented conscientiously to the best knowledge of the writer. Any insinuation or inference drawn from the pages of this book which suggests otherwise is in the domain of the interpreter. I am human, bound with imperfection. In fact, to expect perfection from my narrative is to request the impossible. I will only take responsibility for what I say here and not for what people will interpret it to mean. I have written this book primarily to stir up the consciousness of the contemporary generation to actively participate in public service, and I believe this book will offer immeasurable value to its readers.

**James Useghan**
2019 Senatorial Candidate
Ondo South Federal Constituency

# CHAPTER ONE

# EARLY LIFE AND
# ITS CHALLENGES

Growing up was rough. You obviously needed to be rugged to survive in the ghetto - where I grew up. Life was tough, to say the least. Many were born with golden spoons, some silver and, while others rubber spoons. Having to think of the type of spoon I was born with would lead me into an endless voyage into the land of imagination. The spoon was absolutely peculiar. I am in no way trying to project my background as the worst that any human being could ever possibly experience. So, I would leave the best description to your imagination.

I hail from a typical slum of Ese-Odo Local Government Area in Ondo State- a minority Arogbo Ijaw kingdom, which is an oil producing domain in the Niger Delta region of Nigeria.

Now, when you read of an oil producing state and you try to connect it with the presumable exaggeration in my earlier statement, it seems contradictory.  Such paradox is the reality of the environment I hail from  "poverty aplenty!"

The Niger Delta is the delta of the Niger River breasting directly the Gulf of Guinea on the Atlantic Ocean in Nigeria.

The region extends to about 70,000 sq. km (27,000 sq. mi) and makes up 7.5% of Nigeria's land space. It is typically considered to be located within nine coastal southern Nigerian states, which includes all six (6) states from the South-South geopolitical zone: one state, Ondo, from South-West geopolitical zone; and two states, Abia and Imo, from South-East geopolitical zone. Of all the states the region comprises, only Cross River is not an oil-producing state.

The Ijaw people, being the first to find a settlement in the lower Niger and Niger Delta, might have started inhabiting the region as far back as 500 BC, possibly. It is said that wherever there is a river, an Ijaw born is not far off. Although this is not always the case, yet those words hold great significance.

The Ijaws are a collection of people that are indigenous to the Niger Delta in Nigeria. Owing to their love and affinity with water, a good number of them are found as migrant fishermen in camps as far- west as Sierra Leone, and as far-east as the Gabon. With a population of over fourteen (14) million people, the Ijaws are unarguably the most populous tribe inhabiting the Niger Delta region, and arguably the fourth largest ethnic group in Nigeria.

Historically, it is almost impossible to give a precise account as to whence the Ijaws originated. Different accounts have been given by different historians. But what is certain is that the Ijaws are one of the world's most ancient people. They are believed to be the descendants of the autochthonous people or ancient tribe of Africa, known as the (H) ORU. The Ijaws were originally known by this name (ORU). At least it was what their immediate neighbours called them.

Notwithstanding the fact that this was a very long time ago, the Ijaws have retained and maintained the ancient language and culture of the ORUs. However, language and cultural studies indicate that they are related to the founders of the Great Nile Valley civilization- complex (and possibly the lake Chad- complex). They migrated to West Africa from the Nile-Valley region a long time ago.

The Ijaws were among the first people in Nigeria to have contact with Western Europeans. They were active as go-in-betweens in the slave trade activity of visiting Europeans and the peoples of the hinterlands, particularly in the era before the discovery of the anti-malaria drug, quinine, when West Africa was still known as the "White Man's Graveyard" because of the numerous deaths caused by Malaria epidemic.

Some of the kin-based trading lineages that arose among the Ijaws developed into substantial corporations which were known as "houses". Each house had an elected leader as well as a fleet of war canoes for use in protecting their trade and fighting rivals. The other occupations, common among the Ijaws, are still the traditional fishing and farming.

Being a maritime people, many Ijaws were employed in the merchant shipping sector in the early and mid-20th century (pre-Nigerian independence). But with the advent of oil and gas explorations in their territory, some were employed in that sector. Other main occupation was to be found in the civil service of the Nigerian states of Bayelsa and Rivers, where they are predominant.

Some thirty-one million people, of more than forty ethnic groups, including the Bini, Efik, Esan, Ibibio, Igbo, Annang, Yoruba, Oron, Ijaw, Ikwerre, Abua/Odual, Itsekiri, Isoko, Urhobo, Ukwuani, Kalabari, Okrika, Ogoni and Obolo people, were among the inhabitants of the political Niger Delta, speaking about two hundred and fifty different dialects.

The Ijaw language consists of two prominent groupings. The first, which is known as either western or central Izon (Ijaw), consists of western Ijaw speakers: Ekeremor, Sagbama (Mein), Bassan, Apoi, Arogbo, Boma (Bumo), Kabo (Kabuowei), Ogboin, Tarakiri, and Kolokuma-Opokuma (Yenagoa). Nembe, Brass, and Akassa (Akaha) dialects represent Southeast Ijo (Izon). Buseni and Okordia dialects are considered Inland Ijo.

The second major Ijaw linguistic group is Kalabari. Kalabari is the name of one of the Ijaw clans that resides in the eastern side of the Niger-Delta (Abonnema, Buguma, Bakana, Degema, etc.) which forms a major group in Rivers State.

I am of the Arogbo extraction of the Ijaw nation, a minority kingdom in the present-day south-eastern Ondo State. My progenitors, the founding ancestors of the Arogbo, were immigrants from Ujo-Gbaran town in the 14th century. After a brief stop-over at Oproza, led by Perebeinmo, they went on to Ukparama (now occupied by the towns of Akpata, Opuba, Ajapa, and Ukpe). They stayed there for some time, about the length of the reigns of two Agadagbas (military priest-rulers of the shrine of Egbesu). They then moved to the present site of Arogbo. From this place these descendants spread out to found the Arogbo Ebe.

It was from Arogbo that some ancestors migrated northwards up to the old course of the Forcados river and, thereafter, settled near the site of Patani. Living nearby in the upland region were Proto Edo or Efa people called Erowha. These our ancestors later on intermarried with them and gave birth to the Uvwei and Effurun (Efferun or Efferu who were the ancestors of the Effurun or Ephron, the descendants of Gbaran) sections of Urhobo people. During the time of the expansion of the Benin kingdom (1550), the Benin invaded Ukoruama (Lagos).

The Arogbo sent soldiers to defend the Ijo living in that region. Their army camp became known as Idumu-Arogbo later shortened to Idumagbo. The Arogbo soldiers also successfully halted the advance of the Benin army into the western delta and, subsequently, the whole of the Izonlbe. The foundation of the Arogbo Ebe was done clearly pre-14th century. The ancestors of the Arogbo lived at Ujo-Gbaran between 700 and 1100 AD. Along with the ancestors of the Gbaramatu and Tuomo, they moved to the Escravos region, while the Arogbo ancestors moved further west.

Historically, the Arogbo have had trading contacts with neighbouring Ijaw tribes (Apoi, Egbema) and the Ijebu and Ilaje Yoruba. Most Arogbo people are bilingual, speaking dialects of both the Yoruba and Ijaw peoples. After the death of King Perebeinmo Ogbonu, the founder of the present-day-Arogbo Ijaw kingdom, his son Tabaimotimi Perebeinmo succeeded him as the "Agadagba" of Arogbo Ibe Kingdom. During his reign, the kingdom expanded with the establishments of many towns and villages.

King Barakumoh Perebeinmo succeeded his brother, with the royal title, Perebeinmo III. He moved the headquarters of the kingdom from Ekpetoron to a newly founded settlement then called Arukara-Igbo (Canoe carving land but is now called "AROGBO." His Imperial Majesty, Pere Defaye M. Ebenezer Eperetun (Kukuru), a prominent modern king (Pere) with the title "Aagah II" ascended the throne after sixteen (16) years divisive family misunderstanding.

His reign was characterized by rapid development of the kingdom. A good number of additional schools (both primary and secondary) were established during his reign. In 1981, he was recognized as a first class Oba (Pere), which conferred on him some special privileges, including permanent membership seat in the Council of Chiefs in Ondo State. He played a very vital, prominent and progressive role in the creation of Ese-Odo Local Government with headquarters at Igbekebo. This feat was achieved during the Administration of General Ibrahim Badamosi Babangida .

However, the demise of His Imperial Majesty, Pere (King) Ebenezer M. Defaye Eperetun (Aagah II), in the year 2007, brought about another protracted and wasteful centrifugal inter-family and intra-lineage crises, which evolved into court battles that lasted a period of some twelve (12) years.

His Excellency, Arakunrin Oluwarotimi Akeredolu (SAN), the Executive Governor of Ondo State, rose to salvage the situation. He brought the monarchy interregnum to a close by the emergence and appointment of High Chief Prince Barr. Doubra Zaccheaus Egbunu (JP), The Ibe Bibitonwei of Arogbolbe kingdom as the new Agadagba of Arogbo Ijaw Kingdom on the 4th day of June, 2018.

Therefore, Doubra Z. Egbunu succeeded his brother, King Ebenezer Defaye Eperetun, as the tenth (10th) Agadagba of Arogbo Ijaw kingdom, with the title of "Opukutu III."

Our history brings a serious concern to my heart. We are blessed with the land that can be described as the "wealth pot" of the nation- a land flowing with natural endowments of fortune - the golden egg. Ironically, albeit sadly, within its domain, are people living in squalor and abject poverty, and having a bleak future. They, presently, seem more like inconsequential people of no class and of mean standing. The people seem to have been impoverished by the monster of mismanagement. Such paradox is hard to believe but it represents the reality of our plight. We only wish it has all been a dream!

Another contributing factor to this deplorable standard of living is the abject poverty in the homeland of Niger Deltans, resulting from decades of neglect by the Nigerian Government and the oil companies operating there in spite of the continuous and profitable petroleum explorations in the region since the 1950s.

The December 1998 All Ijaw Youths Conference crystallized the struggle with the formation of the Ijaw Youth Movement (IYM) and the issuing of the "Kaiama Declaration". In it, long-held Ijaw concerns about the loss of control of their homeland's resources and their own lives to the oil companies were brought to the fore and with a commitment to commence an appropriate action to address the situation. In that declaration, and in a letter to the oil companies, the Ijaws called on the companies to suspend operations and to withdraw from all Ijaw land.

The IYM pledged: "To struggle peacefully for freedom, self-determination and ecological justice."

It prepared a programme of action that included with the following:

- A campaign of celebration, prayer; and
- Direct action 'Operation Climate Change' beginning from December 28, 1998.

In December 1998, two warships and some 10 to 15,000 Nigerian troops occupied Bayelsa and Delta States as the Ijaw Youth Movement (IYM) mobilized for Operation Climate Change. The Federal Government soldiers entering the Bayelsa State capital of Yenagoa announced that they had come to attack or hinder the operations of the youths who were trying to stop operations of the oil companies.

In the morning of December 30, 1998, some two thousand young people marched through the streets of Yenagoa, dressed in black, singing and dancing. These soldiers opened fire on them with rifles, machine guns, and tear gas, killing at least three protesters and arresting twenty-five others.

After a protest march demanding the release of those detained was turned back by soldiers, three more protesters were shot dead, including Nwashuku Okeri, Ghadafi Ezeifile and Onwinkron Ibe.

The head of the "Yenagoa rebels"- Chief Onwinkron Ibe- was burned alive in his mansion on December 28, 1998. Amongst his family members who were able to escape from the building that was completely destroyed was his only son, Desmond Ibe. The military declared a state of emergency, throughout Bayelsa State, imposed a dusk-to-dawn curfew, and banned all kinds of group meetings. At the military roadblocks, many local residents were severely beaten with a good number of them detained. At night, soldiers invaded private homes, terrorized residents, beat them and with some women and girls raped.

On January 4, 1999,some one hundred soldiers, from their military base at Chevron's Escravos facility, attacked Opia and Ikiyan, two Ijaw communities in Delta State.  Bright Pablogba, the traditional leader of Ikiyan, who came to the river to negotiate with the soldiers, was shot along with a seven-year-old girl.

Possibly, a dozen of others lost their lives. Of the approximately one thousand people living in the two villages, four people were found dead and sixty-two others were still missing, months after the attack. The same ravaging soldiers also set the villages ablaze, destroyed canoes and fishing equipment, killed livestock, and destroyed churches and religious shrines.

Nonetheless, "Operation Climate Change" continued apace, and it disrupted Nigerian oil supplies throughout most of 1999 by turning off the valves of the oil pipelines that passed through Ijaw territory. In the context of the serious conflict between the Ijaws and the Nigerian Federal Government (together with its police and armies), the military carried out the Odi massacre, killing scores, if not hundreds of Ijaws.

Recent actions by the Ijaws against the oil industry have engendered a renewed waves of non-violent action and militarized attacks on oil installations but without human casualties to foreign oil workers, despite hostage-takings. These attacks were usually as a result of the non-fulfilment by oil companies of the terms on the Memoranda of Understanding agreed with their host communities. The non-ending conflict has seriously and adversely affected the deepening of western education among the people of that territory and increased the rate of criminal activities in the region.

From my early years, I realized that I needed to grow above the circumstances around me, if I must make it big in life. Seeing that my brethren had allowed the destructive environmental circumstances to define their lives and future angered my spirit. I quickly decided to intensify efforts to surmount the seeming insurmountables and to defy all odds in order to break the jinx. It was very difficult because my family was also not immune to that ingrained homogeneous quagmire.

I consider it appropriate, at this juncture, to unveil the background picture and the chemistry of my immediate family. I am from a polygamous family, the fourth child of my mother and the fifth in the family. My father married two wives, and my mother being the first one. She is a fashion designer. My stepmother is late. Altogether, my father has ten children. My relationship with my immediate family was convivial. My experience as a product of polygamous marriage was not a good one. There was always serious misunderstanding of a sort or a quarrel among the polygamous partners, as if they were battling for supremacy among themselves. Consequently, there was always disharmony, discord and the absence of peace in the family.

You see, living in a squalid environment with little or no understanding among members of the family and the apparent lack of parental control were big challenges to many. You cannot have two captains in a ship. The ripple effects of a polygamous struggle were also palpable among my siblings. It was either one was lying against the other or engaging in some unnecessary and avoidable disagreements. These kept fueling the embers of discord, distrust and disharmony in the family. It was altogether an unpalatable experience.

I must, however, admit that the whole drama had some positive effects on me. It made me to be more resolutely determined to succeed in life and to be well focused in the pursuit of my dream.

My father couldn't finish his education during his time. But naturally, he wanted his children to have formal education and be better than him in life. He tried all he could, as it were, but many odds were against most of his children. Apart from the foregoing, the scarcity of the needed financial resources, coupled with the pressure from the environment, were so intense such that they combined to derail the ambition of most of my siblings. And they lost focus.

Due to this monstrous reality, many of my elderly ones couldn't make it to the university. This was the case with most of the youths in my peculiar generation. On the gender flip side, you would find out that promising young and brilliant girls got hopelessly impregnated by notoriously bad guys.

We had an endangered youth- generation, untrained, unsaved and uncultured, with a bleak future, and with some presently still rampaging in the murky waters of impoverished life.

The reason is not far-fetched. After attempting JAMB a few times without success to gain admission to any tertiary institutions, the "wolves" (jobless and irresponsible boys), would come around with all kind of mischiefs, subtleties and deceits, to seduce the hapless girls into 'out-of-wedlock' copulation.

Before the dusk gave way to dawn, the girls would begin to experience obvious signs of pregnancy, the bad boys would have absconded, thus leaving such girls devastated, helpless and hopeless. With some exceptions, it could only take divine intervention for some of such girls to redeem their live and be reintegrated back to the society. This is one way these devious vultures had successfully bred many unfortunate babies, who lacked parental care and love, only to grow up, roaming the streets and increasing the population of hoodlums and irresponsible folks in the society. Most of the hoodlums would begin to terrorize the society by engaging in crime, including raping, robbery and kidnapping.

Some of my siblings were swept away in the ocean of these horrific circumstances. They succumbed to the conventional dictates of the neighborhood, and got impregnated. However, some of them were fortunate enough to be able to bring their husbands to their parents and then got married properly and legally. When Providence chooses to smile on you, gratitude should not elude your heart. But, when you run before your time, you may finish without anyone applauding you.

Early in life, I quickly decided I was not going to get myself fixed into such conventional mold of crime, inglorious life and a bleak future. I decided I was going to chart my course to a successful and glorious future, fueled or driven by strong determination and discipline. I promised myself not to engage in any romantic relationship until my future was secured. Resolutely, I was determined to throw all my energy and resource into what I believed was best for me - education.

I knew I had to pay heavily for my decision. It was not going to be that easy to navigate through the mountainous circumstances around me. But I was convinced about the reality of life and the certainty of one fact: that in order to wear the crown, one must be ready to pay the price. I was so resolute and nothing could change my decision.

My primary school education started in the year 1990 at Umoru Memorial Primary School, Lagos. I stood out in my primary school days and I later became head boy. I competed and advocated for good leadership, even without the consciousness of what I was doing and what I would be canvassing for later in life. Whenever I was asked, "What would you want to become?" I just told them, "I wanna be President of Nigeria."

My naivety couldn't align with the reality and the contradictions around me. All I wanted was peace and a radical change. Somehow, in my naivity, I felt I could change anything with an executive power of the President.

Oil exploration in my land had been on-going long before I was born. Ese-Odo/Ilaje used to be one Local Government Area until they were split. Today, they are still connected by waterways. The development in Ilaje region was second to zero.

Ese-Odo, as a community, had suffered and is still suffering from lack of potable water to date. Presently, the people use water from the same source of supply for bathing; for cooking; for drinking; and for other possible oft-times benefits in the communities. I do not know if God's generous gift of crude oil is a curse or blessing. This is because this God's gift has adversely affected the community by the way and manner it has been explored and extorted.

Recently, some former agitators threatened to return to the dangerous days of militancy, if the government would not come up with a lasting solution to the myriad of problems confronting the nexus of related communities.

Reminiscing on these memories, and the possible resurfacing of militancy, kidnapping, robbery and incessant violence, I still felt the same passion, the unquenchable drive within me, to champion a radical change. I might not have profoundly understood the powers and demands of the President then, but now I know better.

However, I might, possibly for some reasons, want to step down the ambition of vying for the office of the President for other realizable political offices.

For my secondary education, I attended Surulere Secondary School, Lagos where there were more brilliant students from private schools with excellent results than I had expected. On the average, there was a reasonable mixture of the "knows" and "know nots". I blended sharply with my new environment and competed strongly with the best of the best. It wasn't long before I was numbered among the best.

In my final year in secondary school, I was nominated as the food prefect. This was a position that endeared me to many of my colleagues. I used that platform to always help my poor colleagues who had nothing to eat. And whenever I was called to taste every meal, it gave me the opportunity to get some of my friends to visit the food vendors and eat. It was fun for me and, of course, it became a way to assist those in need. I was also the president of Interact Club.

My sheer determination, diligence and hard work duly paid off at school as I graduated with a very good result. It was a dream that came to reality. The excitement was palpable in my family, most especially with my father, who made me vow to earn a degree. This was more of a way to compensate him for his deflated ego; and to boost the family image through the production of a university graduate.

As a young boy, with a sincere intention to be the golden son of the family, I had asked my father what he wanted from me. He eloquently demanded of me to be a university graduate. He said that he was not going to be unduly worried about any chance of getting a job afterward nor would he be disturbed about my course of study. He said all he wanted was a degree. I could almost not come to terms with his seeming ridiculous desire, but, more than anyone else, I understood the depth of such expectation. To him, it was personal and emotional.

Along with my father and everyone else at home, the excitement of my academic brilliance and beautiful grades soon faded into thin air.

Endless expectations, the scriptures say, crush the spirit. After several unsuccessful attempts at JAMB, culminating in six (6) years of futile efforts, the future appeared bleak. Although I was offered admission into Polytechnics, yet I wasn't going to accept anything less than the university course. I had to preserve the sacredness of the promise I made to my father. It was either a university degree or nothing. There was no "plan B" for me regarding this issue.

# CHAPTER TWO

# HIGH SCHOOL AND TRANSITION

An adage says when life doesn't get easier, one has to rise up as a man and get going. While I was still in secondary school, I had learnt to earn extra cash to augment the little I got from my parents. Things became more difficult when my Dad lost his job. As a fashion designer, mum took up the responsibility of sponsoring my education. I was not so comfortable seeing her go through the rigors of working tirelessly alone. I subsequently took up an additional responsibility for myself.

Banking on my talent as a vocalist, I got a job with *Fun-train Party World and Balloons*. The manager, Mr. Austin Chukwuji, had discovered me at a school get-together party, where I went to perform. Subsequently, he invited me to become a member of the band. Weekends became a blessing to me, as there was always a show here or there. I performed with the team at our respective slots and got paid for it. Knowing what was before me, it wasn't too difficult for me to save most of the earnings I received.

With time, I started paying my school fees before getting same from my parents. In fact, I was one of the few that consistently paid their fees ahead of the school resumption date. I also got most of the things I needed for school quickly. Though my parents used to reimburse me for my education expenses, I believe the practice really helped me in two major ways.

First, I was able to focus intensely on my studies and was able to meet other needs. I had to work hard to fend for myself. My academics became more of a personal pursuit and I realized that I had to excel to complement my diligence in combining academics with non-academic activities, which were not an easy task. But it was a must for me and I was really determined to pay the price.

Secondly, I had developed an interest in music through the influence of my elder brother, Michael Useghan. He grew up with my uncle at Ikeja and mixed with some "butty" children. So, when he came home for the holidays, he would sing and rap. I loved to see him do those things and I soon developed an unquenchable thirst to rap like him. The feeling of every weekend engagement in music, coupled with my passion for it, became an impetus to develop my talent in music. It was a confluence of passion and profit; and they all flowed naturally through me.

At some point, working with "Fun-train Party world" was no more lucrative, because expenses were rising and I needed to do something more to get additional funds. I spoke to my uncle to employ me as a conductor for his commercial vehicle, and he consented.

Within the two months I spent working for him, I received quite a number of commendations and compliments from passengers who believed I did well and acted politely. Some were even magnanimous enough to let go of their change to me.

Some of the passengers also advised me to return to school, that being a conductor was not good enough for me. In Nigeria, people generally see conductors from a biased perspective. They believe they are young people without a good future. Some others see them as vagabonds, thugs or thieves in disguise. They are often written off and are never expected to amount to anything in life. So, when people began to persistently persuade me to quit my job, I could understand and also reason along with their concern and genuine interest in me.

Initially, I ignored all the sermons and the pieces of advice to dissuade me from the work. All I cared about then was the money I was making. To me, it was more important to keep the soul and body together with the money I made than anything else. I believed the ends would justify the means. Eventually, I couldn't do the work beyond two months. But the lessons I learnt in those two months has since then become a repertoire of strength for me, from which I constantly draw.

My uncle was also tired of hearing what had become a daily sermon from almost every passenger, advising him to disengage me in order for me to pursue my education. He was greatly disturbed and inundated with the persistency of their unsolicited advice. It was obvious my days with him were already winding up. There was a particular funny event that, I believe brought the whole story to an abrupt end. I had intended to quit working for him on an agreed Sunday evening in order for me to concentrate more on my studies.

On the Friday that proceeded the agreed Sunday, I was diligently doing my work when I saw a young, beautiful lady that I had long admired. She boarded the bus. I never could summon the courage to ask her out. I was overwhelmed by shame and soaked in embarrassment for allowing my "crush" to notice me as a conductor. So I went straight to my uncle and told him I was going home.

He couldn't believe his ears; the shock was noticeable all over him. Rather than anger, I thought, it must have been a surprise that gripped him. He bashfully enquired why I wanted to go home suddenly. I quickly lied that I wanted to go and do some assignments. After a few seconds, in which I felt he had regained his composure, he said "but James, today is Friday, this can wait; more so, that we have agreed that Sunday would be your last day working for me".

His comment deflated my passion to "scamper" from my desire. He won the argument but I decided not to shout for passengers to maintain my integrity with the young lady.

Funmilayo (as I later got to know her name) alighted at the market bus shelter to get some things for her mother. I didn't collect the normal bus fare from her; and that day brought my working experience as a conductor to an end.

Later on, I decided to create an entertainment brand for children, similar to what we were doing at Funtrain Party World. Just that, this time around, I wouldn't be singing. I would dress like a clown and play with children to make money. You see, creativity is a powerful tool in the industry.

You must know how and when to use it.

There were notable professional clowns in the entertainment industry that were found in more popular areas of Lagos State, like Ikoyi and Victoria Island, than many other places in the metropolis. These clowns entertained and played with kids during birthday parties. The kids enjoyed their time, while the clowns made their money. I realized that such was not in place in our local schools, because people felt it was expensive. All the same, I started; and within a short time, it became an acceptable business that created wonderful memories for the kids, while I also made some money.

While waiting for admission into the university, I engaged in a series of works in the area of teaching to stay afloat intellectually. I did not want to end up conquered like one of those street thugs in my neighborhood, impregnating young ladies as their normal practice. I refused to conform to that sordid conventional behaviour. I wanted to be a responsible person. So, I was determined to be successful notwithstanding what it would cost me within the confinement of my moral and religious upbringing. I was not going to accept defeat. I was also not prepared to give up on my dreams.

I literally became a Jack of all trades. I courted the favour of many proprietors, proprietresses and head teachers of schools.They became my dependable clients, always calling for my services to teach. Owing to my congeniality, I was loved by most pupils in schools where I taught.They often begged for my attendance at any given school program. That gave me so many opportunities.

At a particular time, I received an offer to be a permanent school teacher in one of the private schools. But when I got to know the salary that they were willing to pay for my services, and weighing it against the prospects of other offers arising from other activities, I engaged in to augment my earnings. I discovered that accepting the offer would not be in my best interest. Consequently, I settled to be taking only evening classes. Altogether, I taught for about two (2) years while awaiting admission.

Life, as we know, is not a bed of roses, neither is it bread and butter affairs. All I had to do was to faithfully take each step towards the direction of my dream even though the stairs appeared obscured. "An idle hand is a devil's workshop", as they always say, I was not going to free my hand enough for the devil to manipulate for his noxious ventures. Man had to put all hands on deck to achieve his aims.

As much as I was engrossed in teaching, I never abandoned my music passion for a day. I kept fueling my passion, consciously searching all around for every available opportunity. I attended some music talent hunts within the country. I was never shortlisted for only God knows why. But while trying, I succeeded in assisting my brother who was shortlisted for one of the biggest reality music talent hunts, in the country- "The Star Quest, in 2006".

It was a dream come true for my brother, though he never really thought he was going to be shortlisted. While putting in for the music hunt, I suggested that my brother and I should participate in the contest separately. I believe that by doing that, we would improve our chances of being shortlisted and that, at least, one or both of us could be shortlisted. Luckily he made the list.

My brother is a powerful melodious singer, coupled with the fact that he is also exceptional in playing the drums. I advised he should focus more on the drums than on singing, as a strategy to brighten his chances. Eventually, that came out to be his winning ticket.

I must admit, I was excellent with my vocals too, but my choice of songs was not convincing enough for the judges (KC Presh, et al) to consider me. They settled for my elder brother, because of his good strikes on the drum set. At the end of the contest, success smiled on us, as my brother's group, 'The star Quest Band (SQB),' finished as the first runner's up, just behind "D'Accord" which narrowly beat them to win the contest. The accomplished feat afforded my brother some significant degree of fame, as his band was tremendously sought for. I was really happy for him and my hopes soared that some fortune was awaiting us in the music industry.

My passion for music was not without some accolades. I did a series of musical albums that gained massive airplay in Nigeria. My first album was released in 1999, with a group of trio called *The School Boyz*. We had massive airplay way back and performed with the defunct Plantainshun boyz, P-square and The Remedies. We went our separate ways when our musical label mismanaged our brand.

To date, we have four albums to our credit, namely: *Man de work* (1999); *4 Real (2002); Morale (2007); and Egberi-Plenty (2012).*

L-R Michael,  Better (Dancer) me, Useghan & Friday Udoh

In 2004, one of the trio (SDC) went solo and this left myself and my brother still active to date. Music has since become the blood that flows through my veins. I am a lead vocalist in my church to date. As the saying goes, "When one finds his passion, work becomes a pleasure."

After the contest, my brothers' group, The Star Quest Band (SQB), tried to set up a meeting with the Organizers of 'The Star Quest' (The Nigeria Breweries PLC) possibly for a contractual sponsorship. Unfortunately, this attempt did not go through as the organizers were only interested in the winners, D'Accord. Like the popular saying, "No one remembers the second best, the first has it all," SQB kept struggling to maintain the fame, while trying to seek better opportunities next time.The rest, they say, is history.

Fortunately for me, after six (6) years of what seemed like endless waiting, I was admitted into the University of Lagos (UNILAG) to study English Language. I was indeed excited. I quickly rushed home to break the good news to my Dad. The joy that overwhelmed my heart that day was unquantifiable.

It made me to understand how one victory can overcome the effects of many defeats in a matter of seconds.

Prior to my admission, I could remember going to church on a regular basis to meet with my god-mother, Mrs. Wemimo Akinduro. Mrs. Akinduro was then the branch manager of Wema Bank PLC at the University of Lagos. She constantly encouraged me in my quest to secure admission. She would supply me with all the necessary pieces of information about the school, and also guided my moves to succeed.

When I told her that I scored 252 points in the Joint Admission and Matriculation Board (JAMB) examination, convincingly scaling the cut off mark for my preferred course - Mass Communication, she was very happy. Unfortunately, my post Unified Tertiary Matriculation Examination (UTME) score couldn't match up with the minimum requirement to study Mass Communication. My only available option was to get a change of course form and settle for what my post UTME score could afford me.

It was a devastating and demoralizing experience! I could not hold my tears, as they uncontrollably flowed to wet my cheeks. Mrs. Akinduro encouraged me to stay focused and not to allow the change of course process to discourage me. She advised me to receive in good faith any course I was offered, with the assurance that I could always change it when I was finally admitted. She was such an amazing woman, a blessing I couldn't have prayed more for. Most times, she would pay my transport fares whenever I visited her office. After many considerations, I opted for English Language and I was consequently admitted. My excitement knew no bounds, but it was short lived. Two months after I was admitted, the Registrar discovered that the subject I wrote in JAMB could not give me an admission to study English Language. My heart quaked like it was going to jump out of my mouth. I was as confused as I felt hopeless. I practically felt as if I had not been given an admission in the first place.

This was a typical moment when men of faith could critically question their God; when creation would query the Creator; when mortal would sue the Immortal. To say I felt bad is an understatement. My heart was totally broken. All hopes diffused in a moment! "What would I tell my Dad?" was the question that dominated my thoughts as it begged for an answer. The man in me was dissipating with every passing second. I looked at our academic system and wept for so many people who would suffer similar fate like myself. But you see, a man is not defeated until he completely loses his grip on hope. Hope, as blurred as a shadow, can revitalize anyone from his lowest state. I never lost my anchor on hope. So, I quickly went straight to my god-mother for a possible solution and advice. I was not the only victim, as some affected students also went to her for a solution. Armed with our credentials, she took up our case before the Vice Chancellor, Prof. Ibidapo Obe.

Luckily for me, the Vice Chancellor decided to reconsider my admission. He checked my file and came up with the option that I could either choose to study a course between History and Creative Arts. I am sure the Holy Spirit directed my god-mother to pick 'Creative Arts' for me. To the glory of the Almighty God, today I am a university graduate.

And all thanks to God and to her.

# CHAPTER THREE

# STINTS DURING TERTIARY EDUCATION

With my admission secured into the University of Lagos, I did not have too many expectations. Rather, I was projected into endless imaginations of how to beat the odds and graduate unscratched in spite of the severity and the fear of the Nigeria's educational system.

Primarily, all I wanted was simply to read, excel, graduate and secure a job in the oil industry.  My Niger Delta background had bred such a mindset in me that suggested my future was tied to earnings from the very natural endowment beneath the soil of my place of birth. Owing to the fact that I had enjoyed the significant era of my adulthood in a rather less civilized area of Lagos State, I had little motivation for the extravagance of a university life, socialization and politics. The environment was almost completely new to me. I was naive and easily mesmerized by the diverse ways of life on the campus.

It wasn't long before my mind began to work as fast as it could. I had to quickly muster both the mental and psychological strength to cope with my new environment. My experience during the post UTME on campus had taught me some valuable lessons. I could imagine the stress and rigour demanded of me to survive on campus.

On the day I wrote my post UTME examination, I had been scheduled to start by 8:00am.The queue was so long that it took me more than an hour and a half before I started. By the time I started, I was already exhausted. The induced fatigue of standing for almost two hours, coupled with the fact that I had come for the examination on an empty stomach, having thought that I would finish as early as possible, drained my strength somehow, I managed to write the examination.

Such was the life I was bound to face squarely. A life where undue stress was a daily dose. I had also met some few candidates who shared with me their own experiences. It was obvious I could not compare secondary school life with the rigour of university's academic life. They are absolutely two worlds apart. My mind was also saturated with the thoughts of how to cope academically with the demands of my eventual course of study.

Despite my natural ingenuity in creativity, I had never once considered the possibility of studying Creative Arts. I had to count my teeth with my tongue and make do with what I believed destiny had offered me. With my experience during the six years of academic interregnum, I had been deeply schooled in the rudiment of self-survival.

The Department of Creative Arts consisted of Music, Acting (directing, script writing, etc.) and Visual Arts, drawing, sculpting, painting, etc., with distinctive syllabus and courses. As a year one student, I had to enroll for all the courses, and, thereafter, opt for the ones which aligned with my interest. On my first day in class, Dr. Bassey eloquently took us through the rudiments of drawing. The class was quite interesting; the lecturer was jovial, as he painted another realm of drawing into my imagination.

Unfortunately, the imagination effaced as fast as it was formed. I had little patience to accommodate the intricacies of drawing. I desired something more engaging and stimulating. I would have easily opted for music, but I wanted something novel. I wanted to break new grounds, aside the ones I was familiar with. I felt I knew more about music and enrolling for it would only restrict my quest for novelty. Acting seems to be my only option. And to major in 'directing' appears to be novel and, more so, it would engage my creativity.

As far back as 2001, I had tested the water for my acting skills. I featured conspicuously in the movie "*Silver Spoon*" which was sponsored by Christian Dior Videos, alongside some prominent musicians and actors like Daddy Showkey, Ernest Asuzu, Daddy Fresh and Uncle P. I acted Damgbeji in the movie. With that experience in mind, I was persuaded that my foundation in acting was solid, and that reinforcing my prior practical knowledge with academics knowledge would make me fly higher.

Creativity is enormously demanding, both mentally and physically. Having to rehearse all-night, and performing during the day was a life I never would have naturally desired.

Other students saw us as nuisances, noise makers, who sang and danced at every available time and space. It was demoralizing to hear such derogatory comments. But those never deterred me. I was rather motivated with the end in mind; as I was pretty sure that the end would justify the means.

There were some fundamental problems I had to cope with. I had heard many rumors about campus life mostly about cultism and the terror they unleashed on anyone who crossed their path. I really did not want to believe I could be a potential victim. There's an adage that says: "Where people claimed they have seen an elephant, they might possibly have seen a rat; and, if nothing else, they have seen something." Those people that fell as their victims must have been as naive as I was.

A particular event that took place in my first week in the Department of Creative Arts was indicative of how fearful I was. I had been attending English Department lectures before I switched to Creative Arts. The class representative, Fasuhan Ibukun, informed me that I needed to be "initiated", as it was the custom of the department. To me, the word "Initiate" was only synonymous to cultism. It took the intervention and explanation from the Head of Department to allay my fears and correct my ignorance. The right word should have been "induction", but they preferred "initiation".

In order to avoid any trouble and incur the wrath of others, I decided to be a "lone ranger" for as long as I could hold myself. I loathed every form of association. I must sustain my "white garment" from being contaminated by filthy and bad influence. I tried as much as reasonable and possible to maintain a kilometer distance away from every forum of argument or controversy. I thought I should preserve my sanctity.

But then, little did I know that as much as I was running away from trouble, I was as well running to failure with the same pace. I had underestimated the value of positive association. I had forgotten to put into consideration the fact that I was not an Island of knowledge to myself. I needed the eyes of others to see clearly; the ears of others to hear adequately; and the shoulder of others to climb higher.

My first semester result jolted me out of my slumber and delusion! It was an abysmal failure. If somebody had told me that I would perform so poorly, I would have argued and fought the person, thinking that my worst performance could not be as bad, as it were. When I saw a cumulative gross percentage assessment of 2.57, just a little more than average, I was shocked more than I was surprised. There was absolutely something I had missed that I needed to know.

I later discovered that I had ignorantly entered the university system with the naive mind of an innocent secondary school student from a primitive neighborhood. My disconnection from all associations also adversely affected and compounded my trouble. Grading in a university system, most especially my department, was on the merit of the profundity of your answers, reinforced by the relevant references to support them.

During the examination, I saw my mates requesting extra booklets (answer sheets). I was perturbed. By the time they requested for extra answer booklets, I oft checked my own to discover several unused and empty pages beckoning for writing attention. I could not understand what they needed those additional sheets for. I was simple in my approach and, unfortunately, there was no one close enough to deliver me from my ignorance. I thought I was very lucky to have been taught the rudiments of answering questions convincingly by Dr. Otun Rasheed.

Another factor that, no doubt, contributed to my abysmal performance was the demand of businesses I was forced to undertake in order to keep the soul and the body together. University is unlike secondary school where the only acceptable clothing is uniform. On the campus, one has to look good and "smell" nice. It could be intimidating when you see your mates exotically and exclusively dressed, especially ladies with designers' wears and expensive make-up.

Over everything, I later realized, albeit at a costly prize, that academic excellence is the primary purpose of being in the system. I wish it wasn't that late before I knew that. Well, an adage says, "It is never too late than late." It was my first semester, and I knew I had many more semesters to prove my cerebral worth and capability.

Then came the scandalous rumours about students obtaining marks and getting academic grades through the backdoor. They were mostly female students who were alleged to be offering their bodies in exchange for marks. Also, there were some others who were alleged to be bribing their ways through the system. The rumours discouraged me, feeling that the system had been compromised in favour of those lazy students who had corrupted the system.

How could one then successfully compete fairly in a game whose rules were subjective and seriously compromised?
How could anyone claim excellence in a system that was contemptible? How can one diligently burn the mid-night candle in a process one was uncertain of its outcome?
How can one maintain his sanctity in a habitat of corruption?

These might be rhetorical questions in the minds of several people, who might have been unfortunately trapped in the similitude of my predicament amidst system failure.

As I later got enlightened on campus realities, I became more conscious of things happening around me: such as the lovebird meetings that took place at every available garden and space; evening tutorials and religious house fellowships; and got to reckon some, nostalgic "butty", as I prefer to call them, who travelled home every weekend to meet their parents for financial "refueling". I obviously didn't have such privilege, neither did I enjoy such luxury because going home for me was literally a waste of transport fare; that is if I were lucky enough not to part with the little money I had, to support the family.

So I was better-off staying back on campus than going home, even during the holidays. I never attended any school fellowship on campus as I preferred my family church, Christ Anointed Kingdom Int'l Church. As a lead vocalist, I ministered gloriously at the church services. At some point, the church paid my tuition. I knew I was surely indebted to the church, and I continued to be useful in the sanctuary as an instrument in the hand of the Lord.

The General Overseer, Rev. Dr. B. I. Omomukuyo, has since then become an inspiration and mentor to me. I could feel the aroma of his unceasing love for me. He is fondly called "Daddy Shepherd", while I was referred to as "Bobo Shepherd". Our relationship was, and still is, like a father-son relationship. My fidelity to the church together with my piety is sacred. The church groomed me. It is the same church that my god-mother attends. The church members stood by me when I desperately needed help.

There was a particular woman who was special to me in the choir, because she was frequently recharging my phone every month with five hundred naira. In all honesty, the recharge card was a blessing to me as I used it judiciously to further attract other blessings. I often used the recharge card to remind my helpers of their promises. I was what you can describe as an "executive beggar" because I had to discontinue with my side work in order to focus on my studies.

On my list, I had names of helpers that I called upon monthly to solicit financial assistance. When I asked one person for assistance in a particular month, I won't ask the same person again for another three (3) months or more. The style became a routine habit in my four (4) years on campus. Although, my parents contributed their best financially, but their best was nowhere near the minimum funds that I required to meet my expenses. Somehow, I felt that it was only those who had such an experience, a similitude of my predicament, that would understand.

That was the only way to finance my academic pursuit, though I still had my music career going well. In my six years of staying at home, I released two albums in 1999 and 2002. These two seasons gave me the opportunity to meet quite a number of people. I was not really politically inclined; but, then, the lyrics and contents of my music were a mixture of gospel and socio-political issues.

While I was still struggling with my university admission, I got fully into music with my elder brother, Michael. Before then, I had learnt the rudiments of song composition and outright singing. I could easily adapt and do things without much stress. This, I thought, was an inborn gift. And as God would have it, my god-mother never hesitated when she decided to pick Creative Arts as a course for me in the University.

Prior to the time we went to release our third album, we had released a single titled "Same Water". It was a song that was designed to expose the ills of the society in the Niger Delta region of Nigeria. The song gained a good airplay in Nigeria and it facilitated our meeting with some top people who were agitating for better deals in the Niger Delta region. We never knew the impact the song made until we met with Dr. Chris Ekiyor. He was then the National President of the Ijaw Youth Council (IYC).

When I met with him, I had no premonition that he was the same prominent Dr. Chris Ekiyor that I had heard much about. My acquaintance with the renowned National President of the Ijaw Youth Council significantly influenced my political life and perspective on the Ijaw leadership issue. He was a young, energetic, humble, smart and intelligent man. He intellectually engaged the Federal Government during the era of late President Umaru Musa Yar'adua, who initiated the Amnesty programme. Dr. Chris was a fearless and dogged fighter. He was daily exposed to so many dangers. But, with consistency and unwavering spirit, he did survive and he is succeeding.

As we got more and more familiar with one another, I became his loyal disciple and follower. He inspired me with his uncommon audacity. I decided to become a student under his political tutelage. He has since then become my political mentor. Inspired by his political activism and advocacy, I decided to test my wings in the air of campus politicking and unionism. But then, in 2006, the Authorities of UNILAG abolished student unionism.

Favourably, my set in 2006 became the new breed to start student unionism but we came under stricter operating rules and conditions. Although we had no Student Union Government, yet we operated at the Faculty and Departmental levels.

I was in year three (3) when we learnt that the Student Union Government would be reinstated. It was rumoured that the unionism would first operate at faculty and departmental levels. Then, department of Creative Arts was at the verge of becoming a faculty due to its complexity. But in practical terms, the department still remained under faculty of Arts. However, with the large students' population and the many branches of the department, the university management decided to allocate a whole building to house the department. So, Creative Arts operated thereafter more like a faculty. We felt that we were in our own world.

As the rumour gained more ground that students unionism would be reinstated, my conviction of Niger Delta struggle got more solidified. I became more and more resolutely determined in my political pursuit. Understanding all of those challenges made me to be firm in my dealings. I became famous in my department that everyone started to describe me as "militant". Dr. Chris saw the passion and decided to mentor me. He also advised me not to allow my political activities impact negatively on my studies. He shared with me his undergraduate experience, a one time student union President of the great University of Benin, to resharpen my focus, while advising that I should never let my eyes from my primary assignment.

Right from that point, the going seemed to be tough. My results were getting better, but my extra curriculum activities were also taking their toll on me. I met with Dr. Cornel Onyekaba, who I fondly called my daddy. He was a concerned citizen, who persistently showed interest in the Nigeria project. Dr. Cornel lectured on Theater and African-Caribbean in the Department of Creative Arts. He brought African countries together with students of Creative Arts moving round and celebrating African-Caribbean cultures.

Afri-Caribbean Festival was an annual event at the University of Lagos. The campus was often charged turning the atmosphere into a fun-fair and celebrations for art lovers and students who stormed the various roads on the campus. They were engaged in energetic dance, filled with excitement and wore colorful Nigerian and African traditional attires of different tribes. Others got dressed up in traditional attires identified with Brazil, Jamaica and China in the celebration of what was called the "African-Caribbean spirit".

To many people, they saw it as an annual celebration. But to the students of Creative Arts, it was a practical examination session with a lot of financial commitment.

In the lead to the reinstatement of student's unionism at the department, Dr. Cornel encouraged me to contest for the election as he believed I possessed the required leadership qualities. He noted how I had demonstrated some good leadership traits which were unknown to me. He said he had been observing me from a distance. He concluded that I should either contest or become irrelevant. I was caught between the lines. There was the cost implications of running for an elective office; but, on the other hand, I had promised my Dad to graduate unscathed. How could I resolve those conflicts enroute my objective?

I was bogged down by myriad of thoughts, counting my teeth with my tongue before making a decision. I decided to make a wide consultation before delving into the pool of politics. I met with Dr. Otun Rasheed; and his conclusion was more of that of Dr. Cornel's position but with different expression.

He mentioned how passionate I was and how much confidence he had in my ability. And he advised me to think little about the financial implications. On one side of my thought, money was just my real challenge to carry out a new republican government. To me it felt like starting with nothing to build something.

I also visited Dr. Chris Ekiyor, but he was more pragmatic in his response. All he told me was "Good luck, you now have a chance to test your dexterity". It seemed all the people that were close to me won't afford me the excuse to back out of the political objective.

One last person and my fate would be sealed. I had to consult my spiritual father. After explaining my position, Rev. Dr. Omomukuyo only smiled with an encouraging word: It is your time to shine and God will take care of your worries. All my fears dissolved as quickly as his words resonated in my ears. I was now ready to enter the ring courageously.

Before I became conscious of what was happening, my roommate (Michael Ishola) who was then the FASA (Faculty of Arts Students Association) President, had spread my campaign across the department. The time was ticking too fast for me. I had to prepare my manifesto. There were quite some numbers of offices to vie for. The constitution stipulated that the President must be a year three (3) student, going to final year.

I was qualified. I only had one opponent, strong and popular, I must confess. He was my class representative. But he would have had to resign from that office to contest. He was prepared to do that.

I could not say that my expectations were high. I knew my opponent very well. He was very popular by virtue of his office as a class representative. Had I known popularity doesn't often win elections, I would have possibly been more optimistic. It was an open ballot election, with the votes cast and counted under the public glare. The result of the election was a shocker, much more than a surprise. The margin was wide enough to daze my imagination, I won 75% of the total votes cast and counted. It was a massive victory for me in what could be confidently described as a free and fair election.

The joy of the victory indeed overwhelmed me. The first person I called after I was announced as the winner was my General Overseer, Reverend Dr. Omomukuyo. I told him that I was now wearing "The shoes bigger than my legs." He laughed and told me to see him. The following Sunday, I went to church to meet with him. I was pleasantly gifted with a huge surprise. He announced me as the National Youth President of Christ Anointed Int'l Kingdom Church. He said it was an instruction from the Lord.

Even if I wanted to refuse his words, I did not think I had the will and courage to refuse the word of the Lord. It quickly dawned on me that the reward for hard work was more work. I faithfully answered the call, and took up the responsibility. It was such a great challenge for me; the demands were enormous.

I considered that era as formative for me. The National Youth President was a position I held for seven (7) years. It was indeed an experience!

As we settled down after the election, we had to hit the ground running. One project I considered as a priority was the rehabilitation of the road that led to the Department's building. The road was terribly bad, and whenever it rained, students found it difficult to come to class. The infrastructural facilities were not complete but the school authorities had directed that we should move to the building. I believed it was a noble call for me to find solution to the problem, having always been convinced that leadership was all about solving problems.

But then, we needed cash to successfully run the administration. We could not start the collection of dues from students. It was strange to them and we had to earn their confidence and obtain their conviction that the association was constituted to serve them, before we could approach them for financial support. We had to source externally for funds to keep the wheel of the administration rolling.

I ran to my General Overseer for financial aid and he gave me Thirty Thousand Naira (NGN30, 000.00). It was good to start with, but not enough. I started thinking of how to multiply the money received.

I spoke to my executive members, and made it clear that I won't run a dictatorial administration, but give them autonomy within the ambit of the constitution. I encouraged them to be active, innovative and creative in the affairs of their respective offices. I specifically requested to seek financial assistance through their individual support. I told that they would receive twenty percent of whatever they brought to the table in order to run their respective offices. As the first republic student union in UNILAG, we were not paid any allowance, and the expectation was on us to maintain stability and peace.

As we progressed in running the administration, the time came for us to organize a public seminar. We had invested very huge resource in putting up the event. Expectations were high and we could not afford to disappoint the students and the public. I decided to invite Dr. Chris Ekiyor as the keynote speaker. As a former Students Union Government President, and the President emeritus of Ijaw Youth Council, the name Chris Ekiyor commanded awe and respect from many. However, only a few of the people had physically come into contact with the face behind the name. It was a fiercely charged atmosphere in the Niger Delta at that time. And I thought bringing Dr. Chris at that auspicious occasion would certainly make a huge impact on the campus.

About a month to the programme, I personally called Dr. Chris to inform him of the event. He accepted our invitation to the programme. He promised to attend. And he did come with his team. His presence flavored and dynamized the event. It was a massive success. The applause and accolade I received after the event boosted my morale and encouraged me to do more. My name made a round on campus. My two favourite lecturers, Dr. Otun and Dr. Cornel, were so proud of me and were pleased with their instinct for endorsing and encouraging my ambition. It was a great moment for me!

Afterwards, the general feeling of most people was that the Creative Arts Department wasn't meant for just dancers and actors alone, but also to serve as a platform to produce leaders at the national level, who would bring about positive changes in the nation.

James Useghan was identified as one of them. We had several programmes as I gave my all to the Creative Arts Department's leadership. The truth is, I had to pay the price of leadership: I broke down twice and was rushed to the hospital for stress-induced fatigue. But, I came out stronger each time. I have always thought that leadership is a call to responsibility and service. I have never seen it as a platform for self-enrichment, or personal aggradisement, but to enhance the wellbeing of the people.

Another remarkable event we had was the Awards' Night. It was more remarkable for me as I could recollect the event. Due to stress, I was hospitalized on the morning of the day of that event. But miraculously, I was able to make it to the hall around 1:00am, amidst standing ovation. They saw nothing but passion in my style of leadership.

There, I was awarded the "Outstanding Leader of the Republic Student Union". To the best of my ability, I left an indelible footprint on the sands of time. Till date, the Creative Arts Department has my portrait in the department.

Little did Dr. Chris know that he had tremendously and greatly impacted my life. He also had enlightened my path and brightened my horizon. Although he wanted me to pursue my music career, yet it was the "fire" I caught from him that was then the driving force of my life. He was very happy to receive the news about my admission and he was also very supportive of it. But, then, I soon became one of his ardent followers, attending along with him several seminars and symposia at different fora.

At every occasion, I listened with rapt attention, as with others, whenever he spoke. He is given to speaking passionately and eloquently. He introduced me to the lives and times of some prominent Ijaw people such as Late

Jasper Adaka Boro, Chief Ekpemupolo Tompolo, Asari Dokubo and Super Comrade Joseph Evah, all of whom are icons and strong voices in Niger Delta activism till date.

Those experiences collectively and cumulatively opened the eyes of my understanding which helped me to identify with the suffering of my people in Ijaw land. My blood pumped with passion and patriotism for my people. I became committed to the cause. I began to lend my voice to the Niger Delta struggle. My dress code also changed. I approached my mum to make some good Ankara outfit for me with a face cap to go with it (a typical Ijaw outfit). I became a brand ambassador. You could not walk around the Faculty of Arts and miss my Ankara outfit. The outfits also brought some fortune to my mum's business.

It is amazing how people could change overnight. I strongly believe that lack of motivation is what makes people to become complacent regarding their ability. Before I met Dr. Chris, I was fearful and got easily intimidated. Now, my close association with him has made me become bold, strong enough to speak up, to identify actively with the struggle for my people's political emancipation. The feeling has been very strong and inspiring in itself. I have also become proud in who I am and who I aim to become. It is felt like as if some great potentials in me have eventually found a channel to express themselves loudly.

I must admit that my newly found passion posed a significant threat to my academics. I missed classes to attend political symposia as far as Patani in Delta State. That notwithstanding, I never missed my class tests. With diligence and perseverance, I later regained my academic balance. My year one second semester gave me a good landing. I found equilibrium among my three competing engagements: my academics; Niger Delta struggle; and my church, having believed that Jesus Christ died for me. I also had a vow to fulfill to my father who earnestly anticipated my welcome back home as a graduate.

During my four years sojourn at the University of Lagos, a lot of waters passed under the bridge. My leadership skill was greatly tested and tried. I got connected to several people who, indeed, greatly impacted, and are still impacting my life. For me, campus experience was much more than frantic pursuit of academic knowledge, although it was my primary objective. I, however, came to realize that education goes beyond the confinement of the lecture halls.

As much as I excelled in my academic pursuit, I was happier having excelled in other areas which I believe would positively impact my future and shape my direction. At the end of my undergraduate studies, life already took a new form in my mind. I have been privileged to learn on the job, and refine my prospects. More than just an accomplishment, I was glad I could confidently go home and tell my dad that I have fulfilled his wish that he now has a University graduate as his own son!

To me, I knew that that feat was not the end. In fact, I did not see it as the beginning of the end. In the words of Jim Collins, in his best-selling book, *Build To Last*, "It was the end of the beginning": the beginning of a new era that would usher me into the realm of abundant potential and prospects, the realm of productivity and overflows." I quickly understood that allowing myself to be lost in the euphoria of the moment would be a great disservice to myself. I said to myself, the future is here, and I must embrace it and harness it to my advantage.

As I awaited the call to serve in the one year mandatory National Youth Service Corps (NYSC) scheme, I decided to engage myself productively. Technology was booming and computer literacy was fast becoming the fashion of the elites. And if I had to strategically position myself for the prospects of the future, I must, as a matter of necessity, be numbered in the league of computer literates. I decided to enroll for computer training.

After I finished my six (6) months training from the computer school in December 2010, I felt sick. By December 22 2010, I started feeling very strange in my body. I was practically immobilized. Things were happening so fast, as I was taken to different hospitals. I had several medical tests. Then, I was diagnosed of "Malaria Numerous." I had never heard of that ailment before. It was strange, my strength had drastically waned. If not for the fact that I was breathing, I would have concluded that I was in the other world.

Naturally, my parents were greatly troubled and distressed. I was not aware of much of the things happening around me, but I could only imagine the troubles my parents were going through. The son in whom many expectations had been placed was at the verge of death. It was like losing one compass in a distant desert and expansive land space. Hope was disappearing like darkness at dawn. I could not but really empathize with them. It was too much for them to process. I was taken to one of the most popular churches in Lagos in search of miraculous healing, as my mum was a strong member of that church.

Somehow, I strongly believed, like the biblical woman with twelve (12) years of issue of blood, that I would be healed with just a word from the man of God. All I needed was the man of God to say, "You are healed", and miraculously I would be whole. Unfortunately, my situation became more hopeless. All attempts to meet the man of God was abortive. We were told to go to the General Hospital to get a medical report instead of a private hospital. I still didn't understand the rationale behind that. Someone was dying and all they could do was to frustrate his life and hope! The church and its team of ministers were unhelpful.

The General Overseer of my church was not in town then, he was out of the country. I couldn't talk until the senior officials of that big famous church took me to one strange place. It was the church of a man that claimed to be the servant of THE MAN OF God in the big church where the ministers were unhelpful. The man tied my hands, he proclaimed it was the devil that was tormenting and disturbing me. I wept bitterly. I was going through some hellish pains. Nobody was nearby to feel my groaning and anguish. My parents must have been running around for other help.

This man prayed, and somehow, I managed to speak. I told him he was not a good person and that he should take me to my church. I started mentioning the name of my General Overseer. I chanted and cried aloud that I wanted to see "Pastor Benson"; I want to see my "Daddy Shepherd." I cried severely without any help or sympathy. My eyes were soaked with tears, and my body became more feeble and fragile. I seriously wished my "Daddy G. O" could save me from the bondage of chains. I needed serious medical attention.

The acclaimed "Man of God" got tired and decided to eat with his team. A lady, his girlfriend I guess, was a bit kind and generous, but the man callously warned her not to set me free. Luckily, I could faintly recollect the mobile number of my G.O at heart. By this time, the supposed servants of the man of God of the big church were playing Ludo game outside their premises; and there was a phone left close by.

With the modicum of strength left in me, I struggled to pick up the phone. It was a sort of victory that I was able to lay my hand on the phone.  That victory, however, would have been short lived if there was no calling air time or call-credit on the phone.

I dialed my "Daddy G. O's" phone number, it rang. I felt a deep flow of hope through my veins as I heard his voice from the other end. I summoned all the remaining energy in me to make a statement desperately saying, "Daddy Shepherd, help me! I am dying!!"

Now, when the man and the supposed man of God noticed that I had made a call with his phone, he slapped me severally but I smiled, for, obviously, the days of his tyranny were numbered.

My "Daddy shepherd" began to make contacts. He got my mother's phone number, and called her. He spoke with my brother; the church began to search for me. In a twinkle of an eye, everyone had heard of my predicament. When my god-mother heard about my travail and how I was inhumanly treated, she cried uncontrollably. I had really been through hell within those days, the memories were horrible. The torment of the unceasing pains, the heartlessness of a supposed man of God, and, worst of all, the abandonment by my parents, it was indeed a bitter experience.

The first person that came to my location, where I was tied and lying helpless in the den of the alleged "Men of God" was my music Director, Revd. MoyinOluwa Olutayo. Herself and Pastor Philip Ileaboya were sent by my G.O to procure my release. They quickly rushed me into her car and headed to the hospital. I felt slightly relieved, but I wasn't sure I could survive the next hour. My hope and strength further deteriorated immensely when we got to the hospital at Ajegunle in Lagos because there was no bed. That moment was horribly demoralizing. I eventually got a bed but my condition got worse. I had difficulty in urinating and tubes were inserted into me to ease and facilitate the process of emptying my bladder.

After a couple of days at the hospital and my situation instead of improving, deteriorated fastly, the hospital decided to refer me to Gbagada General Hospital, Gbagada, Lagos, for better management and with better facilities. The night that I was to be taken to Gbagada General Hospital was December 31, 2010. It was the Crossover Night for believers. I knew my G.O would be in the Church that night, having returned from his oversea trip. I muttered fuzzily, "Please take me to the Church." I felt before considering another hospital that would admit me, there was one last place I wanted to go - my church. I wanted my General Overseer to pray for me. We arrived at the Church premises at about 11.00p.m on December 31, 2011 on my way to Gbagada General Hospital.

I thought that I had fulfilled my dad's dream and it was time to go to heaven. All the struggles of this world appeared to have come to an abrupt halt. There and then, I wanted to lay down the baton and meet my Lord with a warm smile. The pain was so severe. And when we got to the church, my General Overseer anointed me and said, "You will not die but live." Those were the last words my ears caught as I passed into syncope.

When I regained my consciousness, I found myself in a private hospital around Oshodi. I was ignorant of my location. I could not recognize anyone around me,. A pipe was inside of me, I was on heavy drips. I was later informed that my kidneys had packed up. I was told that the reason for moving me out of the Gbagada General Hospital to the Oshodi Hospital was because there was no dialysis machine available for my immediate use. I was sustained by dialysis machine, while the plans were underway for kidney transplant. My mentor was ready to foot the bill. Several other tests were carried out on me in the preparation for my medical journey abroad.

But prayers by the Church and its members continued ceaselessly, both day and night. It was after the final tests that something absolutely miraculous happened. It was unbelievable, but as real as the palm of my hand. Even the doctors could not believe the results. After a few days of my admission at the hospital my two kidneys started working again. They defied all medical explanations and postulations. Indeed, it was an act of God. How could one explain it better? It just pleased the God of "CAKIC" to make me whole and to live again, by His mercy.  Forever, I shall be grateful. I also appreciate the unceasing prayers from the church and many who pleaded my case before God.

In those few months that seemed like eternity, I went through hell. It was an unpalatable experience. At a time, I was confined to a wheelchair. Right before me, my life seemed to be vanishing away. I was helpless. All my dreams and aspirations were fading into thin air. I didn't know what to think or expect. That I would survive the period appeared to be day dreaming. I missed my school convocation; could I ever even think about that? I was battling with my life; that was the only thing that mattered to me at that time!

At the special thanksgiving service offered to praise God on my behalf, Dr. Cornel and Dr. Otun Rasheed came to my church with many students. They brought me a special graduation gown to celebrate with me and there and then hosted a party on my behalf. I will forever be indebted to them for their kind heartedness. The memory still glows in my heart. I cannot adequately account for all the kind gestures I received. But, I am strongly persuaded that humanity can still thrive in this wicked, callous and barbaric world.

I later found out that the first medical bill that was paid before treatment could commence was settled by a woman I never thought liked me. I knew her from afar, but I was uncertain of her disposition toward me.

She, it was, Dr. Yemisi Ayinde, who made a deposit of a hundred thousand naira on January 1, 2011 for my case and sake. I don't know how I will thank or appreciate her. My Church also paid seventy thousand Naira for my dialysis machine usage. Only God knows what would have been my fate without their timely intervention. I cannot help but hand her and members of my church over to the same God for repayment.

In the words of the Apostle Paul in his letter to the Galatians, his, I paraphrase: "And let Dr. Yemisi Ayinde and a host of others be not weary in well doing: for in due season they shall reap, if they faint not."

The Lord will repay all of them for what they did for me. For if the Lord expressly declares Himself as God of recompense, and He faithfully rewards every sower, He will much more repay those who do good works in multiple folds.

# CHAPTER FOUR

# YOUTH POLITICS:
# FIRST MASSIVE LITERATI (FML)

Prior to my health's travail, I had hoped and anticipated the experience of the one year mandatory National Youth Service Corps Scheme, otherwise known as NYSC with much eagerness. I had dreamt and looked forward to the regimental nature of the twenty-one days camping programme. Also, many stories had filtered into my ears about the rigor of registration, early morning meditation, drilling exercise, military parade, primary place of assignment (PPA), and community development service (CDS). All these brought me mixed feeling of expectations and soberness. Albeit, I looked forward to the experience.

When my call up letter finally came, the doctor told me it was medically inadvisable for me to go for the camping programme after my discharge from the hospital and I was still looking feeble and weak. I was responding appreciably to post-hospital admission treatment and recuperating very fast. There was no way I could have coped with the rigor of travelling and camping. I was posted to the confluence state of Kogi.

The National Youth Service Corps was introduced in May, 1973 after the Nigeria civil war. The scheme was created to foster national unity and integration, particularly among the Nigerian youths. It was also designed to promote ethnic understanding and religious tolerance that were severely impaired as a result of the civil war. The core objective of the scheme was "reconciliation, reconstruction, and rebuilding" the nation. Nigerian graduates (university, mono-technic and polytechnics) are to be posted to states other than their states of origin, where they are expected to interract with people from different ethnic groups, social and family backgrounds, and to learn the culture of the indigenes of those locations.

With the assistance of my elder brother, we managed to travel to Kogi State to seek redeployment on health grounds. I couldn't move out from the car. I was stressed and with my strength vastly draining as a result of the rigor of the journey. I was too weak to do anything. When the NYSC welfare officers saw my condition, they told us to leave immediately. They couldn't phantom how I managed to get to Kogi State and survived in that condition that was exacerbated by the effect of the bad roads.

Before we left, I got registered. I received all my service kits and uniforms (Khaki trousers and shirt, jungle boots, sneakers, white shirt and shorts and two pairs of socks). I was also paid my first monthly allowance. It was always paid in the camp). Then, I completed all the necessary paper documentations for my redeployment to Lagos State on health grounds. It was very impressive and fast. As it was getting late, the authorities were kind enough to provide us accommodation for the night. And early in the following morning, we left for Lagos.

The welfare officer, a woman, had instructed me to return after three (3) weeks of the camping programme. She advised me to come with my choice of primary place of assignment (PPA), where I could serve my father land, while being exempted from the community development service, for health reasons. It was a happy but sober moment for me as I regretted that I would miss all my fantasies about life in the NYSC camp. All such experiences would forever be a dream to me. All I was expected to do was to go to the NYSC Secretariat every month for my clearance. Well, I thank God for His mercies.

While waiting for the three weeks to pass, I was left with no choice than to look out for a place to do my primary assignment. All I had at that moment was hope with few options. While I was an undergraduate, I knew that Creative Arts was not a course that could make one work in an oil and gas company. But I had prayed fervently to God to give me the grace to work in an oil and gas company so as to fulfill my dream. Immediately, I started making serious efforts to reach out to people who could get me a job in an oil and gas company. I already had some one who had been of immense help since I left the hospital, Ken Etete, the Group CEO of Century Group.

I had met Mr. Ken Etete prior to the time I needed help for my national service placement. He (Ken Etete) heard about my health challenges and the struggle for my recovery. He then invited me for discussions on the issue. During our meeting, he enquired of my health condition. There and then, he decided to offer me a blank cheque, by asking "what do you want me to do for you?" To understand the amazement and surprise that overwhelmed me at that instance, you needed to know the corporate and social status of Ken Etete.

Mr. Ken Etete, presently, owns two Floating Production Storage and Offloading (FPSO), facilities. He was, indeed, a God sent to bring solution to my health challenges. I requested for his help in the launching of my newest album which had suffered much delay since 2011. Mr. Ken Etete sponsored the whole event which was held at Oriental Hotel, Lekki. The event attracted many important personalities, the *creme de la creme* of the Nigerian society. They graced the event with their distinguished presence. It was a huge success. Mr. Ken also presented me with a cheque of two million naira as a gift for my upkeep and welfare. That was the day I knew God thoroughly brought Ken Etete to banish the spirit of lack and poverty from my life.

As a result of his tremendous philanthropic gesture, I did not feel comfortable to approach him again regarding where I could do my primary assignment. So, I decided to try other options. I approached Dr. Yemisi Ayinde and pleaded my case with her. She offered to get a possible connection with Total Plc. She had a friend in the company, who helped to take up the issue with someone in the Human Resources Department. But sadly, all efforts proved futile. Time was running out. I knew I had no much choice. I was again constrained to approach my benefactor, Mr. Ken, for assistance. I was not disappointed.

He responded immediately to my request, and spoke to Mr. Stephen Obubo, the then General Manager of Century

Group to place me on a job, no matter the circumstances. I was accepted and employed into the company. I finished my NYSC and was retained in that company. It was a dream come true. I could not but trust more in the divine agenda of God for my life who ordered my steps and stuff toward fulfilling my earnest desires. Till date, with the favour of God aiding every step I take, I got closer to Him (God) and developed more interest in helping the indigents as much as God gives me strength and ability.

Many a time, I had been tempted with solid reasons to quit my job and squarely concentrate on developing youths in diverse capacity. Providentially, my boss, Mr. Ken Etete, also shared the same passion and philosophy with me. He was enthusiastically interested in youths. His fundamental passion was to solve youth problems, empowering people and creating value. He was, and still is, a "youth advocate", who believes that when youths are gainfully employed, there would be less crime in the society.

The sync of passion with my boss made me feel more at home with the Century Group. It was much more than just being a workplace for me. It was an organization where the leaders believed that you could be the best you wish to be and, in that wise, did provide a conducive atmosphere and platform for such development, while counselling that such activity should not conflict with official duties. Such privilege did help me grow rapidly in pursuit of my passion for youth development.

While I was still the National Youth President in my church, I began to organize leadership seminars and workshops to train and equip youths in the church to take societal responsibility at various levels and degrees. My passion grew more and more in fervency with my desire to create positive change in the society. One Sunday, my General Overseer (G.O) was on the pulpit preaching and I could see the holy anger in his spirit. He spoke regretfully about how the youths had been neglected in a society like Nigeria and how only a few were willing to take up leadership challenges in the Nigerian society, particularly with regard to political issues. He admonished and counselled the youths in the church to get involved in politics by joining political parties at early stage in life. He advised them to aspire to become the "now" leaders not the "tomorrow" leaders of Nigeria. He cited a few examples of people who became leaders of their countries at a very early age in their lives: Gen. Yakubu Gowon of Nigeria at 32; Sgt. Master Samuel Doe of Liberia at 29; Thomas Sankara of Burkina Faso at 34; Joseph Kabila Kabange of the Republic of Congo at 30; and General Murtala Mohammed of Nigeria at 37.

There and then, I asked God to show me what to do. Inwardly, I heard a voice saying I should create a Facebook account and call it National Youth Movement. I went to my "G.O." after the service to brief him about my intention and how the Holy Spirit had ministered to me during the sermon. He gave me his blessing with encouraging words and counselling me to be obedient to the divine instruction I had received. Thereafter, I went on to create the Facebook page that same day!

The movement was centered on galvanizing youths to be actively involved in the way our country was being governed and to get more interested in the things happening within and around the country. I believe in advocating for a just and egalitarian society, where the resources of the people are used to satisfy the needs of the people, rather than for selfish and self-serving purposes.

The initiative was conceived to create a progressive, if not dynamic, society built on the principle that a nation is strongest when its youth population works together with a view to ensuring a better standard of living for the Nigerian people.

I am an action man. The moment I received the conviction, I created the Facebook group page in the evening of the same day. The followers in the group increased appreciably, over time. And soon we had about three thousand (3000) followers on the group. We started the registration process with the Corporate Affairs Commission (CAC). We were advised to change the name for strategic reasons. The name National Youth Movement was 'perceived to be political'. The Commission was worried that our intention could create problems for the government.

Consultations were held with the various stakeholders of the group. It was agreed that the organization needed a new strategic name. Then after much discussions, we settled for "First Massive Literati (FML)", as an organization that would provide the platform for massive intellectual transformation for the Nigerian youths. However, this sincere intention did not protect us from the usual antagonism that most organizations of this nature had suffered in the past.

We had several challenges when we were just setting out,

because many youths believed that FML was being sponsored by the Federal Government in order to use them for acts of thuggery, sabotage or election manipulations or, at best, to score cheap political point, and later dump them. A lot of questions were asked and some rumored that the government had given me a large sum of money to carry out some political manoeuvres. Those challenges caused some setbacks, encouraging some youths to leave the group at some point. But at the end of the day, most of them came back, having been convinced by our constant reassurance that the Movement was not a government-sponsored political organization. We made them realize that the group was a genuine youth organization, established to provide a platform for Nigeria youths to become more responsive and sensitive to issues of importance to the country and her youths.

Our maiden official meeting was held online, in a designated WhatsApp group. After that, we started to hold meetings across the states of the federation. We had our maiden physical meeting in Ibadan, the historical capital of the defunct Western region, and political capital of the present Oyo State. However, the first official national meeting was held in Lagos, during which we had some central national executive members elected. The event was covered by some media houses across the country.

It is also worthy to mention that we had youths from eleven (11) states of the federation, converging in Lagos for the maiden national convention. We had youths from Oyo, Kogi, Kaduna, Abuja, Kwara, Anambra, Edo, Delta, Bayelsa, Ondo and Lagos States. They came because they saw the genuineness of the vision, the sincerity of purpose and their belief in the cause for a better nation.

They sponsored themselves to the meeting venue, Faculty of Arts, University of Lagos on the 6th of March, 2017. They provided accommodation for themselves and were also responsible for their participation expenses, covering the whole period that they stayed in Lagos.

Our first national physical meeting was a huge success by all standard. My mentor, Mr. Ken Etete, was on hand to address us and, also, Barr. Tayo Fapohunda. Mr. Ken Etete, during his session, made a remark that keeps resonating in my mind, up till today. He said, "We must create a system that will help the government without the government necessarily knowing." It was indeed a punch-line that became my favorite statement for many months.

The first national meeting was anchored by our highly resourceful national publicity secretary and a strong believer in FML ideals, Mr. Michael Ogunsina. He was also the Oyo State Coordinator. He held on to that position as the Oyo State Coordinator until he relinquished that position for another great supporter and believer in the FML cause, Comrade Adegoke Faith.

One of the positive outcomes of that physical meeting was the establishment of the internal structures and leadership organogram of First Massive Literati. We went ahead to have more standing chapters in more states of the federation. It could be said that we had a strong presence in all the six geo-political zones of the country.

The core objective of our initiative was to build the community up from its weakest point (grass root), and to empower the poor, especially the vulnerable social groups in the society, to achieve a better standard of living for them.

Part of the initiative was to stimulate the growth of the economy through a galvanized and well-motivated workforce in order to achieve sustainable development for our nation.

We knew the imperatives to achieve this goal, including the need to have quality and free education, sustainable health care delivery system, and employment for the teeming youth population. These are very fundamental to achieving our objectives. Those and many other reasons were the motivating factors in our desire to advocate, form synergy, and collaborate with other entities, in order to build a just and egalitarian  society that would give equal opportunity to all Nigerians.

We were of the opinion that it is the responsibility of the government to provide basic amenities for the citizens that should include road infrastructure across the country, portable water, and stable power supply and to ensure the security of life and property within Nigeria's borders. Government should also ensure food security through the use of modernized technology and technologically driven agricultural revolution, provision of decent but cheap ownership housing scheme for the people.

We also felt that a responsive Government would ensure a safe environment for the nation's population by combating environmental degradation and pollution, good system for disposing industrial wastes and boosting the life expectancy of the citizens.

It was our considered view that, by building the youths, who are the strength of the nation, Nigeria would be able to competitively stand shoulder to shoulder with other countries of the world, in terms of economic development, innovation, creativity, science and technology. But in order to achieve these, the fight against corruption must be sustained; security must be enhanced, while the law enforcement agencies must be well-equipped. The Judiciary must be reformed and provided with adequate facilities in order to be able to carry out its function. The military must ensure their independence and non-partisanship in the new Nigeria of our dream.

Our strong belief is founded on our conviction that a progressive country must have productive and vibrant citizens, ready to work and make necessary sacrifice. Basically, we are influenced by what we see, what we hear and the people we interact with. We believe that life is 30% nature, and 70% nurture. Becoming a Literati is by induction and the purpose of the induction is to encourage and motivate the inductees to work with a team that is geared towards making every system that controls our society work. Our desire was to have a team that would create sanity in every sector of the economy and governance, by extension.

It was our intention to develop a system that would set in motion the process of grass root development by equipping and injecting our members with the solid progressive mindset of integrity, accountability and honesty. We also intended to organize training, capacity building workshops and empowerment programs that would produce leaders that would transform Nigeria, without political violence or social conflict.

The Movement began to grow rapidly in strength and in number. I had to travel across almost all the States of the Federation, including the Federal Capital Territory. I organized the various chapters of FML while sharing the vision, the mandate, and the drive with students of different campuses, in many youth organizations, online and offline. I attended radio interviews to share my passion with media audience. I also issued press releases to enlighten people of the youth the passion that had become a sort of personal ambition. It was really a daunting task but like I did with my life and health issues, I did not give up!

During the last general elections in Nigeria, the FML members, from different states across the nation including myself, stood and bore flags of different political parties. Many of our members, leaders and stakeholders contested for elections in Kogi, Lagos, Ondo, Ebonyi and other states of the federation: and in all fairness, considering the level of rottenness in the Nigeria's political space, we did pretty well.

In one of my discussions with the FML Coordinator, Osun State, Mr. Adeniyi, he stated: that "President, with all due respect Sir, I love this vision. But do you know that to gather ten (10) youths in Osun State is a big problem?" He continued, "Let me tell you, Mr. President, there is no source of livelihood, no jobs, and many schools are often on strike. Personally, as a state Coordinator, I sometimes find it difficult to meet my personal needs; things are so hard for the youths."

My heart burnt within me, when I thought about the plight of our youths. Most of them live a life of depravation, neglect and hunger. Those who were working did not have enough to cater for their families, due to the hardship in the land. Many were found roaming the streets from dawn to dusk in search of elusive employment. The condition was really terrible; and no one with a good conscience would pretend or feign ignorance of that reality. Many were already losing hope and giving up on the Nigeria dream. I listened to a conversation between a brother (Delta State Coordinator), Mr. Theophilus David, and another friend in a forum, where the latter vehemently but frustratingly said, "Nobody can change Nigeria!"

The statement brought a chilling feeling down my spine. I became apprehensive and tormented with fear. I was afraid, not for what he said, but because of the fact that the guys would have influenced a lot more people with such negative and pessimistic assertion.
If all of us would allow our hope and strength to be swept away by the sordid reality of the moment, then the future was going to be disastrous.  Somehow, I also decided to share my concerns with others. I shared some of the concerns publicly but not without an optimistic conclusion.

In 2017, the Movement, through its national executive body, planned for a National Economic Summit. The summit was designed to bring together youths from all walks of life, in about twenty-three States of the federation, including the

Federal Capital Territory. The idea was for the organization to brainstorm on the issue of proffering feasible solutions to the economic problems of the country.

The summit also brought together opinion leaders, economic gurus and accomplished technocrats from all works of life.

The publicity for the summit was extensive and massive. But, just like every other non-governmental initiatives, the major setback and constraints of the summit was the lack of adequate financial resources. The movement engaged a public funding strategy to raise money for the summit. This strategy proved to be very effective. Although, the turnout was considerably poor, much more, the emphasis of the campaign was for every State chapter of the movement to organize itself and ensure a reasonable population presence and attendance at the summit in the University of Lagos, Akoka.

The build up to the summit was a mixture of stress of varying degrees and frustration. Some of the members of the organization worked tirelessly round the clock to ensure the success of the summit. We had a list of notable speakers, whom we had invited. A considerable number of them responded positively, while some were unavoidably absent. One of them was Mr. Fela Durotoye.

When I met with him, it was obvious he wouldn't be able to make it to the summit. He had another important engagement scheduled for that day. He apologized, but to show his commitment, he decided to make a video presentation of his speech to be streamed live at the event. I commended and appreciated him for his commitment.

Due to the paucity of funds, one of the strategies that we employed to publicize the summit was through social media platforms. We banked on the strength of our population and individual network of friends to give adequate pubilcity for the summit. Though we also made use of some traditional publicity means of communication, such as daily newspapers, radio and television channels, yet more of our attention was focused on digital publicity through WhatsApp, Facebook, Twitter, Instagram, and so on.

On October 20, 2017, one of us, Comrade Ayanniyi Taiwo, wrote about the reason why youths of indiscriminate extraction should participate in the summit. In his words, he said, "If you look critically at Nigeria as an entity or nation, the political stratum is saturated with many anomalies, economy is recessed, infrastructure is jejune, social amenities are in shambles. Practically, nothing is working religiously in this nation. We merely exist, instead of living buoyantly to enjoy the glorious wealth nature has bestowed on us. We have abundant resources, but woed with poor management and leadership skills!"

There is a separation of powers in our nation's constitution; but, due to greed, sheer abuse of power and massive corruption, the line of the separation of powers that should allow for proper accountability, checks and balances among the ties of government has been eroded.

First Massive Literati is a movement constituted by

progressive youths who clairvoyantly foresaw and ardently believe in the bright future of Nigeria. They are young intellectual minds who are ready to commit their energy, time, and resources to gestate and chart an achievable blueprint for a better Nigeria.

The much anticipated ECONOMIC SUMMIT, slated for November 4, 2017, was one of the many platforms created to enable great intellectuals rob minds together in order to birth new ideas, devise postulations, and make reasonable plans to bring about economic renaissance for our great nation.

Diversification is a word that has dominated our political space and various economic gatherings for some time now. Theoretically, strong and strident voices have clamoured for it, but there has not been any pragmatic and political will to actualize it.

Our advertisement slogan and publicity strategy went like this: "As youths, the strength of the nation, let's join and attend this summit to add more echo to our voices. There are already well-meaning speakers and panelists on ground to polish our minds with adequate knowledge on how to revamp the tattered economic system. You can't afford to miss this gathering of intellectuals from across at least 27 states of the federation, including the Federal Capital Territory, Abuja. Be part of the 2017 ECONOMIC SUMMIT @ Unilag's main auditorium, Lagos, Lagos State."

On August 31, 2018, through the blog site https://haderotakisblog.com, I made a statement concerning the 2019 general election. The content of the statement is reproduced verbatim below:

"The underlying expectation from any investment is to generate substantial and complementary results. One should then begin to wonder why despite the enormous providential investment and endowment of Nigeria as a nation, the country refuses to neither be productive nor thrive to complement the magnanimity of nature. Nigeria is unequivocally a nation with the favourable eyes of nature. Providence has smiled on us and we are undoubtedly on the fortunate hierarchy of natural endowments, with some sumptous deposit of every mineral resource that can be found anywhere in the world. The nation can lucidly be tagged the bank of natural resources, a land flowing with milk and honey; yet, there is little or nothing to show for them."

"It is unimaginable to admit that the nation has tarried so long in the rank of an underdeveloped nation, or as some people would like to put it, the only country in the third world. Nigeria, despite being blessed, lacks the leadership and managerial prowess to transform those resources into results. She remains a nation without fundamental social amenities, even at the break-neck speed of technological evolution and civilization. The current state of the nation brings so many aches to a discerning heart. Compared to the giant progression of the rest of the world, Nigeria is in retrogression, with a significant propensity of imminent collapse. There is this evident leadership vacuum that has eaten deep and invariably cut across almost every stratum of the nation's domain, be it private or public sector."

"No one could have captured the deficiency in the leadership echelon of this country better than one of the British colonizers of Nigeria and a former Governor-General of Nigeria, Frederick John Lugard in his book, "The Dual Mandate in British Tropical Africa", where he asserted thus, "He (Nigerian) lacks the power of organization, and is conspicuously deficient in the management and control alike of men or business. He loves the display of power, but fails to realize its responsibility...."

"We have a nation where education - the platform that is supposed to hone and build human capacity with the intention of positioning, consolidating and reinforcing the people to bear responsibility- is treated with outright disdain. Gradually, our educational system is being dangerously discounted with underfunding, lack of basic educational paraphernalia, and diminishing incentives that were they to be copiously available, could have encouraged scholars in their academic pursuit.

The government of the day is ignobly shying away from the responsibility of equipping the coming generation with standard and undiluted education which would have invariably served as an effective tool to change the nation for better. With the regrettable deliberate enactment of policies enshrined in the current political dispensation that is discouraging education in various capacities, one could painfully admit that Nigeria is a tinderbox earnestly waiting for a time to explode.

Currently, the nation is dotted with crops of unsophisticated people at the helm of affairs. We have a country where mediocrity will unanimously win over and above excellence in the court of public opinion. People seek certification rather than competency. Sound academic, professional and experiential qualifications have been substituted and sacrificed on the altar of shenanigans, knavery and pursuit of dishonest gains.

Recently, the country was announced with reference to a global statistics as the most impoverished nation in the world. The ripple effect of this fact is evident and felt in almost every household of the federation, even though our government will somehow deny it with manipulated and concocted figures that do not reflect any positivity on the life of an average Nigerian.

It is so sardonic that those who work diligently and tirelessly in their spheres of endeavours and public service domain will be compelled to go home with nothing or, at best, half salary at the end of the month. People are suffering, aching with the unimaginable fact that a hand that is working isn't getting enough to feed himself nor his immediate family: skyrocketing inflation and high cost of living won't cease to take its toll either.

On the other terrible side of the coin lies a myriad of others, graduates and artisans alike, who despite their potential and proficiency are not able to find gainful employment. They are simply disadvantaged by virtue of their country of birth. These sets of people are celebrated in other climes as they invest their physical, mental and intellectual strength to develop their nations in diverse capacities.

'Contrarily, these bright brains have been technically downplayed, debased and subverted to a mere tool in the hands of political gladiators in order to achieve and perpetuate their mischievous ventures. Leveraging on the high-level of unemployment and impoverished masses, the politicians have subtly weaved a soft-landing space to manipulate the helpless masses, most especially youths, by employing them for devilish acts such as thuggery, ballot snatching, and as propaganda buzzers; and, consequently, making them an easy prey for vote buying.

Another general election is fast approaching and it seems that Nigeria is still where she used to be or, better said, she's further deteriorating rapidly. Politicians are already closing their ranks to rape and rob the helpless and hapless masses as usual. The truth is, the divided interest of the masses has preponderated their will to drive in a transformation mechanism. The politicians are daily sowing the seeds of discord, most especially, amidst the youths, to weaken their collective strength, so as to pave compromising way for their devilish ventures. Yet, the youths won't cease to amaze me by swallowing their stratagem, hook, line and sinker. So unfortunate!

A nation that sacrifices merit, capability, competence, integrity and dignity for mediocrity, shabbiness and sleaziness will eat the fruit thereof.

Nigeria deserves better. We deserve a round peg in a round hole. We deserve people with measurable capacity and competence; people with professional, academic and experience- based sagacity to mount up the throne of leadership.

We deserve individuals that will painstakingly identify the wants and the problems of the people and shrewdly contrive an effective mechanism for solution- delivery. We deserve a better Nigeria.

There are some things we keep denying daily. We keep excusing ourselves from them because they are ideologies we perceived to be perverted. Yet, these things keep confronting us as often as we live. They make us look inferior and second- rated in the comity of nations. Then, we must admit something is wrong somewhere and we should look inward to figure it out;  otherwise, we get drown in our own inactions.

# FML ECONOMIC SUMMIT @ Unilag's

African Youth Leadership Summit

Newspaper publication after the summit

Audience

Audience

Coordinators
Ameen Yahaya, Kaduna
with Mohamed, Niger

## FML ECONOMIC SUMMIT @ Unilag's

Bar. Fapohinda & Ken Etete

Audience

Interview with STV

Ibadan Summit

Oyo Chapter FML

Ibadan Chapter FML

Lagos Chapter FML

Abuja Chapter FML

Ibadan Chapter FML

Port-Harcourt Chapter FML

FML Programe held in Lagos

Delta Chapter FML

Enugu Chapter FML

Niger Chapter FML

# CHAPTER FIVE

# 2019 GENERAL ELECTIONS

Once the ideology of First Massive Literati was set in motion, and the organization began to create a national ripple in advocating good governance, I began to search deeply into myself to consider the next line of action. I was appreciative of the fact that the organization was getting a wide publicity and wider recognition through its numerous ventures, but the satisfaction was not as profound as I would have liked.

Until the power of governance returned to the rightful owners, the majority of the people, most especially the youths, and their productive endeavours are harnessed and integrated into Nigerian's economic system, I believe all our efforts would only amount to merely cutting the leaves, while the roots of the proverbial national tree fester in decadence.

One of my primary aspirations was to ensure that by the time my unborn children come into this world, I would be able to give them a government they could call their own- a government which would acknowledge their peculiarity, bolster their strengths, supplement their weaknesses and engage their resourcefulness in building an all-inclusive, progressive and sustainable system of governance.

I was of the opinion that sitting on the fence and embracing complacency and apathy would not afford me the opportunity of realizing my aspirations. But, strangely I came to realize that I had not really considered throwing myself in the political ring to take the bull by the horns.

Prior to the moment of intensive build up to the 2019 general elections, I was persistent in what I believed was in my circle of influence, advocating through several media outlets, political platforms, seminars, meetings and conventions on the need for active youth participation in government. I had, many times, called upon the youths for the need to develop personal credibility and competence. I canvassed for the need to raise an army of "change makers" who would rise through the ranks to make a transformational impact on our national political landscape.

I thought and believed that the bad precedence of ineptitude, corruption, nepotism and cronyism that has eaten deep into the fabrics of our society, economy, politics and religion should no longer be accepted. And if good, agile, competent and credible people would not rise in the dire moment of time to rescue us from the brewing danger, the chance of redemption might not surface within the next decade. It was for that course that I devoted my time to pursue all as the general elections drew near.

One day, I received a call from Reverend Dr. B. I. Omomukuyo, my General Overseer. He called to inform me that some people from the United States of America would like to meet with me. I was not fully briefed on the subject of the meeting. However, my personal relationship with Rev. Dr. Omomukuyo assured me of positive intention and development. Later, I got to know that my G. O., being someone who was tremendously acquainted with my aspirations, had relayed my desire, advocacy and passion to Most Reverend Bolanle Shonekan, who had lived most of his life in the United States of America. He was then on a mission to contribute his quota to his country's political development and economic vibrancy by encouraging trustworthy youths to contest for elective political offices in Nigeria.

Pa Shonekan is a simple man who believes absolutely in God. He rarely embraced the stress of fanning his own fire or letting anyone do it for him. He just would leave things in God's hands and wait on the Lord to handle every situation that come his way. As he often would say, "If you can just praise God for my life and my mission to help the youths, that will be enough for me."

That is the reason why he has vested interest in the youth. In order to support his stance, he quoted Matthew 19:14, "But Jesus said, Suffer little children, and forbid them not, to come unto me: for of such is the kingdom of heaven." He believed (still does) that the youths are the future of the nation; and that to preserve the future, the youths must also be preserved.

Most Reverend Shonekan told me that it was time to practice what I preached. He assured me of his readiness to purchase electoral forms for as many credible and competent youths, as would be willing to contest against the old and outdated politicians in power. His argument was that to make the right and desired change; the right people must be involved in the process. He was convinced that the youths had tarried long enough, outside the ring, as spectators, it was time for them to get actively involved.

His argument was persuasive and I applauded his good intention. In a country where the "old cargoes" and generals were still dominating the political scene, while their counterparts were suffocating the society with massive domineering attitude. It is most rare to come by people of Most Reverend Shonekan's kind. This reinforced my trust in his intentions and my willingness to yield to the patriotic call.

After our discussions regarding the issue of youths' participation in elective positions, I agreed to contest for the State House of Assembly. But, the superior argument of my General Overseer and Most Rev. Shonekan persuaded me to accept a bigger call to the senate. They insisted that I should aim for the sun, and that even if I missed it, I would still be among the stars as an alternative. They were both convinced that I was most qualified, not only to contest, but also to deliver the profound dividend of good youths' representation. I was overpowered by their compelling and persuasive arguments and the confidence they both reposed in my ability.

Pa Shonekan, as he is often called, being the leader of the African Youth Congress (AYC) offered to get me a form from another political party since AYC couldn't meet up with the deadline required by the Independent National Electoral

Commission (INEC) for registration. He opted for Sustainable National Party (SNP) headed by Mr. Da Silva.

Purchasing the form gave me the practical reality of the event that was to unfold in my life. It seemed like I had been dreaming, but holding the form in my hand jolted me to life. I was at the crossroads of making a critical decision with little or no experience. The only practical experience I had before then in electioneering process was when I contested, as an undergraduate, in my department's union's presidency. Student unionism is quite different, both in content and context, from party politics.

I had never before contested for a ward councilor; but, right in my hand was the form to contest for a senatorial seat of the African biggest nation. It was simply audacious, if not totally crazy!

In one of my posts on the social media at that time, I relayed my concern and aspiration to the public with these words:
"Yes, I am not too young to run. However, it is very obvious that I am too poor to run. It is obvious that I don't have the millions of naira to fund my campaign. It is obvious that over 65% of our youths are jobless. It is obvious that our youths have been rendered desolate and have nothing good to show the world on how to earn a living. It is obvious that the youths of our country are in dire need of someone that will represent their interest'.

'It is obvious that the responsibilities of our parents are getting worse, to the extent that youths above the age of thirty years are still under their parents' houses, begging for 'chop money.' It is obvious that some of our youths might be used again to cause electoral violence. (We will keep advocating, while we orientate them). But, the good news is that a lot of our youths are awake and are alive to their responsibilities to salvage this country. We are tired of running round in a circle. This is one reason for coming out to represent the youths and my people in Ondo South and to pass a national message: the youths are important and relevant. We will secure our future back and keep the flag of the progressives flying'."

That was an audacious statement! I only knew the word; I really didn't know how to translate it into action. I was only certain with my burning passion that I could always proffer solution to any emerging problem. The reality of what to expect before, during and after the elections soon caught up with me.

Many thoughts began to fly aimlessly through my mind. Many unanswered questions were being generated in automation. Daily, I read of the unimaginable struggle of public servants, most especially politicians, defamation of character, litigation, and propaganda, unfounded and ridiculous rumours- all in a bid to sweep away oppositions' credibility and submerge their relevance. I was not sure if I was ready for such dirty game. Another important question was how to source for adequate funds to contest the Nigeria massively monetized elections. I was caught between the thick and the thin line of dream and reality. But, I decided to hold on to hope.

With the electoral form obtained, I rolled up my sleeves to get to work. The first thing was to source for funds. Although

Pa Shonekan had planned to help raise some funds, but after waiting to no avail, I resolved to alternative means. I immediately created a WhatsApp group, added some potential sponsors, people with aligned sense of passion and purpose, who would be able to throw in their fortunes for a just course. I also created a 'Fund Me' account to solicit public funding. But, unfortunately only my donations and two others, who donated five hundred naira each, were received. The money is still there till this day.

Through the WhatsApp group, I was able to raise over eleven million naira for the election. With the financial issues almost settled, we started working on strategies to win the election. I visited all the six local government areas in Ondo south senatorial district. I consulted with all stakeholders, sought counsel from monarchs, community elders, clan heads, religious leaders, political agitators, private and public power brokers that were presumed to be relevant to my political ambition.

We enjoyed a warm reception from the progressives; and those who, like us, were positive and optimistic that Nigeria's future would be great with the youth in power. Anywhere we went, we were also warmly received, with a touch of affection, kindness and hospitality.

But typical of the deplorable state of Nigeria politics, many of the people expected and anticipated to receive from us monetary inducement, instantly. They, more or less, represented people who wanted to eat all their seeds without sowing. I saw them as clogs in the wheels of development, being the very root of our political rottenness and the aches in the heart of sincere ambitions.

The six local government areas in Ondo south senatorial district are as follows: Ilaje, Odigbo, Irele, Okitipupa, Ese-Odo and Okeigbo/Ile Oluji.

According to available statistics, the highest votes from the senatorial district were expected to come from Ilaje. My local government, Ese-Odo, ranked the 4th in our analysis. To get any closer to the Red Chamber seat from the district, we needed to strategically maximize our efforts and resources in order to have an upper hand in the most important local government area.

After identifying and analyzing all the defining political variables at our various strategic sessions and meetings, we launched our political ship to the open sea.

The obstacles were daunting. Our people had been mesmerized to perceive every politician from a narrow preconceived prism. It was a prism that reflected all kinds of politicians that had entrenched themselves into the affairs of the community with money to buy as many votes as possible from the electorate. There were no honourable expectations other than to satisfy their immediate financial need. It was so painful to see that almost everyone was waiting for another four years to roll by so as to share only crumbs and pittance out of their national patrimony. People were willing to sell their votes for as low as hundred naira!(Less than 50cents!)

The reason for this was not far- fetched. Poverty had been politically weaponized to subvert the political rationality of the people. Much more, the people saw every four-year of electioneering process as an opportunity to get back at their political oppressors, and negotiate handsomely to satisfy their ever-increasing hunger for money. It is the best they believed that they could do. Ignorance also contributed immensely to that myopic attitude. Only a few people understood the essence of true democracy and its long term benefits. The system still adversely affects both the electorate and the politicians. It is a cycle of shame.

For one to completely gain true perspective and understanding of the issue, and to be able to judge the situation fairly, one has to stand observantly on both ends of the divide  of the electorate and politicians- in turn.  More often than not, we are tempted to judge the politicians unfairly from our narrow point of view.

The electioneering process, with its heavy monetization consequences, would bring the politicians into financial crises from which many of them would find it difficult to come out. In Nigeria, elections, in reality, involve very huge financial commitment or investment. Many people do borrow or take bank loans and put expensive properties as collateral to access funds. And naturally the politicians would expect returns on their investment.

One can only wonder how many politicians, with good intentions, have got choked up in the system, and eventually become pawns in the hand of their political god fathers. Politics is a dangerous game in Nigeria, sometimes with serious threat to life and property from political enemies. Politicians, therefore, need to secure and protect themselves and families from foes and dangerous elements in the society. They have to spend huge sums of money to secure the services of security operatives, both for themselves and their families. We have heard and read of several cases of politicians or relatives being kidnapped or assassinated, even If it is meant to distract their attention.

Another contributing factor to the huge electoral expenses in Nigeria is the countless and different people that politicians have to "settle" or "grease their palms" in order to secure their support, elicit their understanding or gain their attention.

Often times, people queue at the door of the houses of politicians every day to receive money for 'feeding'. Many politicians are inundated with several invitations to public fund raising engagements from communities, individuals, non-government organizations, religious groups and other similar associations.

 A Nigeria senator once confided in me that on the average, more than a hundred people queued up at his house daily; and that he fed them almost every day. Additionally, he said he often gave out large sums of money.  This might be the major reasons why politicians do become corrupt at the end of the day.

Far from it, I am not trying to justify the excesses and irresponsibility of our politicians. I only offer a robust analysis of their problems. We should not exclude some part from the political equation of corruption and then parochially declare a verdict. We should consider all the variables, analyze them and proffer a holistic solution. The politicians, as well as the electorate, contribute in varying degrees to the sordid state of the political affairs in Nigeria. None of them should be exonerated from blame, neither could anyone of them escape vicarious responsibility for the rot that we see in the Nigerian political system.

During my campaign, I visited many communities where it was customary and traditional for politicians to give cash on plate, because no one would visit the elders empty handed. In most of our meetings, we also had to cater for their logistics, such as transportation expenses; and provide them refreshments. Indeed, I got to realize that politics was meant for the "rich" and economically buoyant people. One does not seem to stand a chance as a poor or middle income earner, as far as politics is concerned in Nigeria. That reality soon became clear to me as a result of my experience on the campaign field. To ignore that truth is to wallow in stack ignorance and the world of illusion.

I believe whatever has gone wrong should be blamed on the rottenness of the system, for which we are all to blame. We have unwittingly and collectively set into motion a system that is hell-bent on destroying us. We seem to be helplessly at its mercy. We have encouraged a "transactional" system of politics, rather than "transformational" to thrive in the country. This is a system that stratifies society and narrowly selects its players based on class of haves and have-not: the system that only answers to "money bags" and currency notes. The only language it recognizes and responds to is money. It is the system that only knows how to share power of influence and affluence: the system of subservience, shenanigans, stratagem and subterfuge. We are all responsible for such self-destruction in the system. Our actions and in-actions have contributed to the whole terrible and unfortunate situation we find ourselves today. We are all to blame!

On the fore, I bluntly made it explicit to everybody that I was not going to buy into such a rotten system. My campaign rhetoric clearly suggested that it was not business as usual. I made it clear, *ab initio,* that I was not going to be part of the transactional politics being practised in Nigeria. I created an impression that suggested that I was ready to work, to be transformational, if the people were ready to give victory to both themselves and myself.

To what extent this strategy was to be effective, I could not say; but, I was aware of the fact that people have naturally fought or resisted change, most especially when it would entail displacing them from their comfort zone. I was certainly persuaded that the gain would be worth the pain.

In all sincerity, I must admit the strategy was effective to a reasonable extent. It was a noble idea, and I wasn't delusional as to expect a miracle. I was pragmatic about the approach. It was a right thing to do by putting a square peg into a square hole! It was my considered opinion that by the persistent drops of such water of change, we would sooner than later have a mighty ocean of the desired change.

I was optimistic but not day dreaming. We only have to get as many people as possible to keep dropping and contributing to the pool, until they form an ocean. I thought that my audacity of hope should be given a chance to thrive.

With the campaign drums fully rolled into space and place, we began to gather people in small and large numbers. In many of the communities we visited, we were assured of support and votes. But I knew, as most politicians do, that what matters most was the day of election, when those individuals who had promised their support would stand to cast their votes, to make the deciding choice.

I was aware of the fact that there were many factors that could sway opinions; and promises before that crucial moment, a final decision would be made. To every politician, that moment is the most important time.

At some point, I became so confident about the result of the election, because we were receiving goodwill messages and massive support from the youths who had identified with us and had taken us as one of them. The sweeping effect of the prospects of having the youngest senator ever was palpable in the senatorial zone. Most of the young people in the six local government areas were ready to give their all for a young aspirant that would represent the true interest of the people. It was an instructive but interesting moment. We intensified our campaign, journeying through the land and the river, from house to house, creek to creek, community to community and local government to local government. We had many sleepless nights. There was a particular instance where we had to sleep overnight in a big ship in parasitic company of ruthless and ubiquitous mosquitoes.

It was during those campaign travels and visitations that I began to gain profound perspective on the well-being of the people, their needs and desires. I didn't just see people that were in dire need of radical change, I also saw how my people have been neglected for so long, without any visible sign of development. In the whole of Ondo South, there was no evidence of power supply. The land was in perpetual darkness all the time. No potable water in many parts of the local government areas. They were virtually lacking in most basic amenities, which people in other parts of the country would have taken for granted.

I began to wonder what the previous representatives and public office holders had been doing. I thought that either they never intended to represent the people or they totally misrepresented them. We began to devise, formulate and think about practical solutions to those problems with a view to mitigating the sufferings of the people. We were not ready to leave the slightest thing to chance. I still held to the basic truth that public service means work, and to work effectively one must plan in earnest. The people needed good leadership and proper representation. And if we were to fill that gap, and make a difference, our strategy must be made to address those issues that would radically transform the lives of the people and positively impact their living condition.

On January 1, 2019, about two months to the general elections, I made a statement published in the Sun Newspaper, regarding my commitment to join others to make laws to improve Nigeria's economy, if elected. In one of my consultative visits to the sectional National President of Ijaw Youths Council (IYC) world-wide, Mr. Oweilaemi Pereotubo in Warri, Delta State, I had relayed to him my intention, not just to represent the interests of Ijaw nation, but also to ensure that I sponsored economic bills that, if implemented, would stimulate economic growth and solve the unemployment problem of the country; and even making most Nigerian youths become employers of labour.

Convinced of my intention, he commended my courage, vibrancy and boldness in coming out at such a crucial moment to canvass for the political and economic emancipation of Ijaw nation in the country. He also promised me his goodwill and the support of the Ijaw youths. While wishing me well, he prayed for my success at the polls.

On February 15, 2019, I made another statement which was also published in the Sun Newspaper, page 44. On that occasion, I assured the people that a victory for me would birth many of their dreams that had been long kept in the limbo without any effort to bring them to reality. I promised that the people would see and marvel at the tremendous progress that would be made within a short period of time. I also promised to sponsor bills that would give special attention to the welfare and standard of living of a number of the vulnerable social groups in the society, including the aged, the widows, the physically challenged and senior citizens.

As the elections day drew nearer, we intensified our strategic and open space campaigns. We leveraged on the social media to reach out to the youths. We produced and gave out branded T-shirts; brought in musical bands to mobilize people and propagate our visionary messages. Both community and spiritual leaders in the senatorial zone prayed for our success. Our campaigns brought us face to face with both the beauty and the beast. We encountered the bad, the good and the ugly! One notable of those experiences was when some fraudsters extorted me. It was aching to think of such people. May God deliver us and our country from such evil people.

I was never discouraged by the antics of those fraudsters. Some people would come from another political party to claim that they were ready to work with us, just to extort money from us. At the end of the day, the same people would be seen wearing T-shirts of other political aspirants. I saw them as political jobbers, looking for ways to make easy money and to make ends meet. The evil ones were out to swindle any unsuspecting politician as a way to survive in life. However, permit my confession: the financial consequence of losing money to swindlers was already taking its toll on me. At that point, I knew I needed God the more. There was no money to throw around from my little earnings. The campaign exercise was running out of funds. I was almost going to sell my car, but thank God for my wife (then, fiancée) and two good friends, Ugwu Barnabas and Afeez Ajibade, that stood by me all through the heated electioneering process with unflinching financial support. Other people donated generously to my political ambition also.

As the day of election drew nearer, the concern to raise additional funds to settle polling unit agents began to cause palpitation and mind-weight for me. For us to ensure that votes cast for us were counted and recorded for us, we needed to deploy uncompromising and God-fearing agents to the scene. The logistics involved demanded a huge amount of money.

A day to the election, February 15, 2019, my team had started calling all the agent coordinators for each Local Government Area to appeal to them and to give them a token for their logistics support in each polling unit. We agreed to give to each unit a token sum of two thousand naira.

The amount was nothing compared to the mobilization fee given by professional politicians who could offer as much as twenty to thirty thousand naira for the same job. We passionately pleaded with the agents. I must, in all sincerity, appreciate those who accepted to mobilize themselves to the polling units from their personal pockets. They were indeed a blessing to us, whose worth no one could quantify in monetary terms.

We had over one thousand polling units. So, imagine giving two thousand naira to each party agent; that is about two million naira. That was a huge amount of money for someone like me! It was impossible to raise such funds from any source whatsoever without expectation of a commensurate return. The reality beckoned and I must commend those who, in good faith, saw our struggle and generously offered to help. It was to further reinforce my belief that, contrary to the popular narratives, our society is still very much enriched with good people.

At about 4am, on the day of the election, precisely February 16, 2019, the electoral umpire called off the game, to reconsider the rules when the game was presumed to have started.

It was a devastating blow to our morale and a shame on our national image. I felt so angry and frustrated. I was practically speechless. No one took responsibility for the ineptitude regarding the financial, political, economic and human resources wasted and all the efforts put into the exercise- all just went down the drain! All that we had was that the postponement was due to some inexplicable logistics reasons. The speech of the Independent National Electoral Commission to that effect is reproduced below:

**"ADDRESS BY THE CHAIRMAN INDEPENDENT NATIONAL ELECTORAL COMMISSION INEC, PROFESSOR MAHMOOD YAKUBU, TO THE STAKEHOLDERS' MEETING ON THE 2019 GENERAL ELECTIONS AT INTERNATIONAL CONFERENCE CENTRE, ABUJA, ON SATURDAY 16th FEBRUARY 2019**

About thirteen hours ago, I conveyed to Nigerians the decision of the Independent National Electoral Commission (INEC) to reschedule the 2019 general elections by one week. Presidential and National Assembly earlier scheduled for 16th February 2019 will now hold on Saturday 23rd February 2019 while Governorship, State Assembly and FCT Area Council elections scheduled for 2nd March 2019 will now hold on Saturday 9th March 2019.

The one-week adjustment was a painful one for INEC but necessary in the overall interest of our democracy. Nigerians will recall that when this Commission was appointed in November 2015, we promised Nigerians two cardinal things. First, we shall work hard to consolidate the improvements made in the management of elections in Nigeria since 2011.

Secondly, we shall always be open, transparent and responsive. We have strived diligently to keep these promises in very trying circumstances.

In keeping with our promise to consolidate the gains of the last two electoral cycles, the Commission has conducted 195 re-run and off-season elections across the country since the last general elections. Most of these elections have been generally adjudged to show progressive improvements in planning, execution and outcomes.

This commitment to continue to improve on election administration has informed our preparations for the 2019 general elections. Our goal is to plan carefully, execute meticulously and bring stability into election management in Nigeria.

Consequently, we announced fixed dates for elections in Nigeria to the effect that Presidential and National Assembly elections will always hold on the third Saturday in February of an election year, while the Governorship and State Assembly elections follow two weeks later.

Having settled this, we began the planning quite early, with a Strategic Plan (SP), 3 Strategic Programme of Action (SPA) and an Election Project Plan (EPP). In fact, the plan for the 2019 general elections was ready in November 2017 and we subsequently issued the timetable and schedule of activities for the elections over one year ago on 9th January, 2018.

We carefully followed the timetable and implemented I3 of the 14 activities as scheduled. We kept to the timeframe and have not missed the date fixed for any single activity.

In preparing for the 2019 general elections, we have come face-to-face with the realities of conducting such an extensive national deployment of men and materials in a developing country like ours. It is said that elections constitute the most extensive mobilization of men and materials that any country could undertake in peacetime.

The challenges of doing so, even under the best of circumstances, are enormous. Within a period of 16 months, we registered over 14 million Nigerians as new voters, collecting their names, addresses, photographs and their entire ten fingerprints. Beyond that, we prepared, printed and delivered their permanent voters' cards for collection. I should note that of the 14.28 million Permanent Voters' Cards (PVCs) made available for collection, about 10.87 million or 76.12% have been collected.

It is often not appreciated the magnitude of activities that the Commission undertakes during general elections. Not only that, we have recruited and trained about 1 million young people to serve as ad hoc staff.

The magnitude of materials mobilized for our elections is enormous. For instance, the Commission has printed 421.7 million ballot papers for six scheduled elections, as well as 13.6 million leaves of result forms for the Presidential election alone.

Indeed, managing 91 political parties and 23,316 candidates for whom votes will be cast in 119,973 polling units by over 84 million voters is certainly astounding.

No doubt preparations for the 2019 general elections have been extremely tasking for the Commission.

It is therefore not unexpected that such a tremendous national mobilization of men and materials will encounter operational challenges and we have had our own fair share of such challenges.

There have been delays in delivering ballot papers and result sheets for the elections which are not unusual. However, I must emphasize that all the ballot papers and result sheets were ready before the elections despite the very tight legal timeframe for finalizing nomination of candidates and dealing with the spate of legal challenges that accompanied it.

In this regard, the Commission has been sued or joined in over 640 court cases arising from the nomination of candidates. As at today, there are 40 different court orders against the Commission on whether to add or drop candidates.

The net effect of these is that there is usually roughly a one-month window for the Commission to print ballot papers and result sheets and either fly or transport them to several destinations until they finally get to each polling unit.

Unfortunately, in the last week, flights within the country have been adversely affected by bad weather. For instance, three days ago, we were unable to deliver materials to some locations due to bad weather.

We, therefore, had to rely on slow-moving long haulage vehicles to locations that can be serviced by air in spite of the fact that we created five zonal airport hubs: Abuja (North

Central), Port Harcourt (South-South and South East), Kano (North West), Maiduguri and Yola (North East) and Lagos (South West) to facilitate the delivery of electoral logistics.

Apart from these logistical challenges, we also faced what may well attempt to sabotage our preparations.

In a space of two weeks, we had to deal with serious fire incidents in three of our offices in Isiala Ngwa South Local Government Area of Abia State, Qu'an Pan Local Government Area of Plateau State and our Anambra State Office at Awka.

In all three cases, serious disruptions were occasioned by the fire, further diverting our attention from regular preparations to recovery from the impact of the incidents.

In Isiala Ngwa South, hundreds of PVCs were burnt, necessitating the recompiling of the affected cards and reprinting in time to ensure that the affected voters are not disenfranchised. I am glad that all the cards were quickly reprinted and made available for collection by their owners.

In Qu'an Pan Local Government Area, our entire office was razed, destroying all the materials prepared for the elections including printed register of voters, ballot boxes, voting cubicles and several electricity generating sets. 11 Registration Areas and over 100 polling units were affected by the fire.

We recovered quickly and have since replaced everything destroyed. In addition, we secured a suitable building from which to conduct the elections.

Perhaps the most serious was the fire incident in our Anambra State Office at Awka, which destroyed over 4,600 Smart Card Readers being prepared for the elections. These Card Readers take at least six months to procure.

Despite this setback, we have practically recovered from this by mopping up every available spare SCR across the country and within 24 hours delivered them for elections to hold in Anambra State.

All these challenges mean that there have been differences in preparations from one State to another. Our overall assessment is that if the elections went on as planned, polls will not open at 8am in all polling units nationwide. Yet, we are determined that polls must hold at the same time everywhere in the country.

In this way, elections will not be staggered. This is very important to the public perception of elections as free, fair and credible. We promised Nigerians that we shall be open, transparent and responsive. Faced with these challenges, we initially thought that we only require a maximum of 24 hours to resolve the logistics issues involved and complete our deployment for the election. This would mean shifting the elections to commence on Sunday 17th February, 2019.

However, given the restriction of movement during elections, that could affect many voters who worship on Sundays. While the Commission was considering the following Monday, 18th February, 2019 as an option, our LCT Department advised us that it would require 5 -6 days to reconfigure about 180,000 Smart Card Readers earlier programmed to work only on election day, Saturday, 16th February, 2019.

It is for this reason that the Commission decided to adjust the election dates to Saturday 23rd February, 2019 for Presidential and National Assembly elections and a consequential adjustment of Governorship, State Assembly and FCT Area Council elections to Saturday 9th March, 2019. Some sensitive materials have been distributed.

However, all such materials have been retrieved and will be taken back to the custody of the Central Bank of Nigeria. I want to assure you that there will be a proper audit to account for all materials.

In the next few days, the Commission will work on the basis of the following plan:
S/No. Activity Time Frame
1. Completion/confirmation of deployment: Monday 18th February, 2019 of materials
2. The configuration of the Smart Card Readers: Sunday, 17th Thursday, 21st February 2019
3. Receipt and Deployment of sensitive materials to LGAs: Wednesday, 20 and Thursday, 21st February 2019
4. Refresher training for ad hoc staff: Thursday 21st February 2019
5. Deployment of personnel to RACs: Friday 22nd of February 2019
6. Election Day: Saturday 23rd February 2019
I want to appeal to Nigerians and all other stakeholders for their understanding of what has been a very difficult decision for the Commission. But we believe that ultimately this is for

the good of our democracy and country.

I wish to assure you of our commitment to free, fair and credible elections.

As Chairman of INEC, and on behalf of the Commission, we take full responsibility for what happened and we regret any inconvenience our decision might have caused.

Thank you and God bless." (End of quote.)

As a person, I was of the opinion that none of the highlighted reasons was logically plausible to warrant the postponement of the elections barely five hours to their commencement time. The Commission had enough time to tie all the loose ends and ensure the elections went on as planned.

The most prominent reason given for the postponement of the election was logistics. That was simply a well-crafted and irresponsible word to hide their sheer incompetence. The Commission was appointed in November 2015, some four years before the election date.

Whatever logistics' problem the Commission could not put in place within that period of time, would certainly not be possible to resolve within a week if we are going to be sincere with ourselves. We all know that there is no smoke without fire. Prior to the day the elections were to commence, there had been speculations and rumours from different quarters that the Commission had been compromised.

However, no one paid serious attention to them, except, of course, the perpetrators and their cronies, who were not bothered about the negative impact the postponement of the elections would have on the global image of the country.

All that mattered to them was and always has been their dirty ambition. They are ever ready to shed the blood of dogs and baboons to ascend to power. One could have easily deciphered the ulterior motive behind the postponement, watching closely the body language of the chief actors.

Peter Ayodele Fayose, a former governor of Ekiti state, warned, through his twitter handle, two days before the elections, that the Leadership of the ruling All Progressive Congress Party was currently at a meeting, considering the postponement of the elections to March 2, 2019, using the burning of election materials in Anambra, Abia and Plateau States, as well as security threats in some other states as an excuse.

I feel it is advisable for one to pay some attention to the self-fulfilling prophecy. The "script" regarding the election postponement was said to have been prepared by the 'Presidential cabal'.

It was totally ridiculous to read the statement made by the Vice President Professor Yemi Osinbajo's spokesperson, Laolu Akande, through his twitter handle, when he said, "Mr. President was already in Daura in Katsina State and the VP already in Lagos to vote this morning before the postponement just announced by INEC.

This is truly disappointing, but the march to the Next Level continues. Nigeria will prevail."  One would not but begin to wonder the depth of conspiracy embedded in that statement for anyone to have boldly claimed that the number one and number two citizens of the Nigeria State were kept in the dark on such a pressing national issue just like an ordinary average Nigerian.   I believe they could fool themselves and their gullible foot soldiers, but not any sensible person.

The situation soon deteriorated to a war of words between the ruling party and the leading opposition party. I believe the official press statements from the Presidency and the one from the opposition party would be adequate here.
They are set below:

"STATEMENT BY PRESIDENT BUHARI ON THE
POSTPONEMENT OF GENERAL ELECTIONS BY INEC
I am deeply disappointed that, despite the long notice given and our preparations both locally and internationally, the Independent National Electoral Commission (INEC) postponed the Presidential and National Assembly elections within hours of its commencement.

Many Nigerians have traveled to various locations to exercise their right to vote, and international observers are gathered. INEC themselves have given assurances, day after day and almost every hour after hour, that they are in complete readiness for the elections. We and all our citizens believed them.

This administration has ensured that we do not interfere in any way with the work of INEC except to ensure that all funds were released to the commission.

We now urge INEC to ensure not only that materials already

distributed are safe and do not get into wrong hands, but that everything is done to avoid the lapses that resulted in this unfortunate postponement, and ensure a free and fair election on the rescheduled dates.

While I reaffirm my strong commitment to the independence, neutrality of the electoral umpire and the sanctity of the electoral process and ballot, I urge all political stakeholders and Nigerians to continue to rally round INEC at this trying national moment in our democratic journey.

I, therefore, appeal to all Nigerians to refrain from all civil disorder and remain peaceful, patriotic and united to ensure that no force or conspiracy derail our democratic development. I have decided to move back to Abuja to ensure that the 14.00 hours meeting called by INEC with all stakeholders is successful."

Statement from the leading opposition party presidential candidate, Alhaji Atiku Abubakar reads:
As you know, the Independent National Electoral Commission has announced a postponement of the elections until 23 February and 9 March respectively.

The Buhari Administration has had more than enough time and money to prepare for these elections and the Nigerian people were poised and ready to perform their civic responsibility by voting in the elections earlier scheduled for Saturday, 16 February, 2019.

This postponement is obviously a case of the hand of Esau but the voice of Jacob. By instigating this postponement, the Buhari administration hopes to disenfranchise the Nigerian electorate in order to ensure that turn out is low on the rescheduled date.

Nigerians must frustrate their plans by coming out in even greater numbers on Saturday, 23 February and Saturday, 9 March respectively. Knowing that the Nigerian people are determined to reject them, they are desperate and will do anything in their power to avoid their rejection by the Nigerian people. Their plan is to provoke the public, hoping for a negative reaction, and then use that as an excuse for further anti-democratic acts."

According to the Punch newspapers, the PDP chairman, Uche Secondus, called on the INEC boss to resign. He said the postponement was a plot by President Muhammadu Buhari to cling to power. Secondus noted that the ruling party having failed in all their nefarious options to enable them to cling on to power, the APC and the INEC came up with the idea of shifting election, an action that is dangerous to our democracy and is therefore unacceptable.

The PDP chairman, in a statement signed by his media aide, Ike Abonyi, said, "With several of their rigging options failing, they have to force INEC to agree to a shift in the election or a staggered election with flimsy excuses pre-manufactured for the purpose." He also noted that, for the avoidance of doubt, the PDP sees this action as wicked and we are also aware of other dubious designs like the deployment of hooded security operatives who would be ruthless on the people ostensibly to scare them away.

All the big players began to throw tantrums, cutting the leaves, while the roots festered in immense decadence without check. That was absolutely not unusual in Nigeria political scene. I wonder how we could claim that we were progressing when we still get entangled in the same trap of history, over and over again!

But that was exactly the argument of some pro-INEC and ruling party stalwarts, arguing that election postponement was not a new thing in the nation; and it was not going to constitute a crime if it persisted. Such is the chronic retrogressive and repressive thinking of some people in the helms of affairs of a nation acclaimed to be the giant of Africa!

Thus, we have people who have refused to take vital lessons from history to heart, so as to benefit from its wisdom, but rather ignominiously repeat it. What a shame!  We keep cycling on the same spot for almost six decades, without much progress to show in terms of physical, mental, political and economic development.

It reminds me of the story of the biblical Israelites who, because of their lack of faith in themselves,  abilities and skills, and their terrible sins of perversion, disobedience to God and recalcitrance wandered in the wilderness, frustrated, in turmoil, underdeveloped, discombobulated, but finally arrived at their Promised Land after forty years journey, though heavily depleted. For us, with the many years in the nation's wilderness experience, the Promise Land is still not in sight.

In a country where no one takes responsibility for national systematic failure, where everyone endlessly blames others, except themselves, and the authorities craftily exonerate themselves, one should expect less or little from such a people.

As usual, the dust died down without causing any fatal damage, most especially on the senior players, only our national resources, the helpless electorates, and innocent candidates, like myself, suffered the bruises in terms of the wasted time, energy and money.  This is more so because quite a number of Nigerians travelled from other countries of the world to exercise their franchise, their businesses impaired, with huge amount of money spent on security and logistics - for everything to go down the drain.

Another awful side of the story, which reflects and further reinforces the miserable state of our system, was the travails of the helpless Corp members deployed for national assignment.

We read different accounts on several social media platforms of how Corp members were stranded in the middle of the night, ill-treated and disillusioned by the sudden postponement of the elections at the dawn of the D-day. Some were forced to sleep, albeit inconveniently, in the INEC offices, while many others were exposed to dangers as they were sent away without any means of transportation in the middle of the night. It was altogether a sad story in the annals of our national electoral history.

It will be an understatement to say that we still have much to learn as a people.  We have much more distance to cover as a nation in trying to imbibe sound democratic ideals and practice. I do sincerely hope that the 2019 elections' flaws do not get repeated in future. We surely need to forestall a repetition of such a disgraceful event in the history of our nation.

With the elections rescheduled for February 23, 2019, all hands were on deck to plan for the best and prepare for the worst. The extended time made us to incur several other unanticipated expenses. We had no option other than to re-oil our machinery and set it in good shape for the D-day. A week is too much for a serious politician to take for granted, because people can easily get swayed and dance to the tune of another party. We had to revisit some of the places we had earlier visited to reassure our people of our commitment so to remain steadfast with us come rain, come shine. We also had to encourage our polling unit agents not to lose faith, and be ever more determined to see the election process through to the end.

On the Election Day, I went to my polling station, Ward 1, Unit 3, Arogbo Local Government Area at about 8, o'clock in the morning. After unceremoniously casting my vote, like many professional politicians did, I waited for a while to observe the electioneering process.  First, I noticed the electorates were forced to keep their phones away from the polling unit. This, I believe, was for no reason other than to prevent the recording of the possible acts of ballot box snatching by political thugs and bandits.

I also received information from reliable sources that some bigwig political party agents were involved in an unwholesome act of vote buying during the voting exercise. The act was said to have been carried out under the "watchful" eyes of security operatives who might have been bribed and seriously compromised. I felt helpless, and incapacitated in the face of injustice. I had no security to guarantee my own safety. I watched helplessly as I was being cheated out of the race. It was a terrible experience. The people were ignorant of the damage they were doing to the system. I could, therefore, not blame them entirely.

Some electorates came to me after the voting exercise to demand for money. I was dumbfounded and perplexed. A particular old woman almost tore my elder brother's dress. She was angry because we refused to give her money. She felt cheated because it was the norm to vote and receive payment. She was very bitter and exasperated. She threatened to report us to her kindred who would forcefully demand what she believed to be her right. I was sorrowful. I left the polling unit with so much aches and pains. My worry was how one could help our people who were being locked up in the ignominy of a bastardized political system.

For a moment, I felt Nigeria was a lost cause; that the thought of better days could only exist in our imagination! Everything seemed hopeless. I was practically overwhelmed for the moment by the system. But I was persistent, I earned some significant votes on merit and that swelled my pride.

I then remembered the word of Mr. D. I. Kekemeike. He said, "James, if one person votes for you, count it as a thousand." That was enough of a success for me, though it did not end there: I lost the election, but I won the sincere votes of people that believed in the future of our nation, Nigeria.

To me, the adversaries of our nation are in the minority, if every well-meaning Nigerian will contribute his or her own positive quota as a citizen.

On the day of the election, I, remembered, a young lady came around to us and was bragging and showing off about the NGN11, 000(Naira) she profited from the dirty game of vote selling. She disclosed that she was going from place to place, selling her voters card to the highest bidder. She appeared to be one of such people that preferred to have a loaf of bread to having a full bakery.

Yet, despite the integrated mechanism of rigging, engaged by my opponents, I won some polling units in Ajapa, Amatibi and some other places in Ilaje LGA. I also received an impressive number of votes in Irele.

Among the fifteen contenders for the senatorial seat, I came fourth after the final counting of votes. All the three parties that were before me were the "heavy weight" parties, with huge resources and wherewithal to manipulate the system and the people in their favour.

I found myself in a contest with people that were not too honourable and would embrace cheating in order to secure victory. Many of them lacked the spirit of sportsmanship. They were ready to soak the dogs and the baboons in crimson blood in order to achieve their devilish ambition.

That I survived the electoral contest was a miracle. My greatest joy was that the votes that I earned were done on merit, without any force, coercion, inducement or intimidation. The people believed that I could deliver the dividends of democracy and be able to represent them responsibly at the Red Chamber.

Every single vote I received is important to me. It signifies hope; hope that the nation stands a chance for greatness; hope that there are still people who are honourable in their conduct; hope that, with persistency, we can overcome evil with good; and hope that someday, our dear nation shall be great!

It was a choice; a noble choice at that, for people to ignore the immediate gratification of vote selling, to vote for a candidate that only offers them a sincere manifesto of what's possible. Having recognized the fact that such people exist and having received their support, I am most joyful that I contested. For I have long ago learned that it is more honourable to lose than to cheat, and to lose merely offers one another opportunity to win overwhelmingly at some other time in the future. I shall wait for that time, and when it shall come, I shall throw my hat in the ring again, much more determined for success than I had done previously.

The election indeed caused me a lot; a lot much more than I can quantify in cash, and in kind. And most painful loss was the death of my immediate sister that occurred three days after the election. It was a rude shock for me. Her death pained me to the marrow of my bones. She stood by me throughout the electioneering period. She cooked my food and made meals for my followers during the campaigns. She worked so hard and took good care of me. After her death, everything appeared meaningless to me. Many people came up with suspicious and superstitious questions while trying to connect her death with the election.

At that point, it was as if my world was crumbling. My mother was rushed to the hospital on hearing of her demise. She had high blood pressure. It was a terrible moment for my entire family. For me, I couldn't come to terms with the reality of her death. I felt confused and emotionally depressed. Things happened too fast. When I was yet to count all my losses after the election, suddenly there came the tragic death of my sister. It was too much for me to bear. I tried to convince myself that all happened for a reason; but such logical philosophical reasoning could not obliterate the emotional emptiness that I felt.

What if I had won the election, would I have been able to celebrate the victory? What would people say? Many of such questions occupied my mind. My thoughts wandered aimlessly. But at the end, I am grateful to God that I could pick up myself from the dust of grief; and being able to move on again. I decided to live once more. I know it won't be easy but it is a worthy choice. My fiancée (now wife) was with me during those trying times. She encouraged me in all the struggles; then we got married seven months after the sad event of my sister's death.

## CAMPAIGN POSTERS

## CAMPAIGN POSTERS

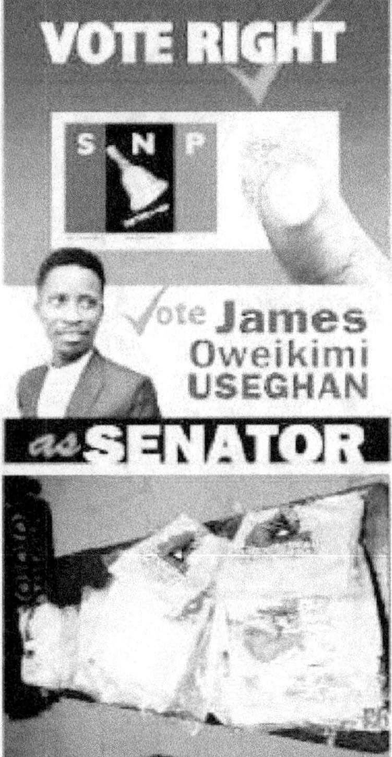

## CAMPAIGN/RALLY

Bolowou Kingdom

Amatibi Community

Amatibi Community

Zion Hall Bolowou Town

# CAMPAIGN/RALLY

Odigbo Community

Odigbo Community

Arogbo Community          Ajapa Kingdom

## CAMPAIGN/RALLY

Arogbo Town

## CAMPAIGN/RALLY

Okeigbo Community

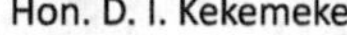

Hon. D. I. Kekemeke

Relatives

Water Front Rally

# CAMPAIGN/RALLY

Odigbo Community

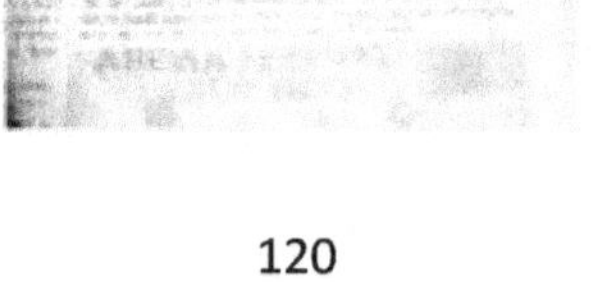

Ilaje Community

# CHAPTER SIX

# LIFE EXPERIENCES &
# THE NIGERIA POSSIBILITIES

In life, if you have a roof over your head, something to eat, and few cloths to cover your nakedness, I believe that you are blessed. You are better and more privileged than so many others who live in squalor. Life has never treated everyone equally, but we all make demands on life by our efforts and pursuits. As we grow and transcend each level of human development, we gather strength, knowledge and skills to make significant and successful demands on life. The process of growth is available to all humans, and I sincerely believe that there are three primary areas that one should earnestly strive at, to gather enough strength, and to receive enough push for significant success in life.

I started out this journey of election contest in real ignorance of the reality of the enormous demands of its process. I had been involved in student unionism during my undergraduate days. But communal politics is quite different. One could not have known better without a trial. I had read about it, heard about it and often talked about it, but getting into the ring myself to experience the process first-hand was a mind-blowing experience.

Initially, for a youth to contest for an elective office in this nation would have literally been considered a mission impossible! With the passage of the "Not Too Young To Run" bill, the coast seemed clear for the youths. But the question we failed to ask then was how would many of our youths get the required financial resources to successfully contest the heavily monetized Nigeria elections?

Perhaps we were looking in the wrong direction; we were made to believe that the Nigerian youths had a chance when actually they had little or no chance. Our chances were tacitly tied to the retrogressive strategy of submitting to the old politicians, as toothless dogs while following them aimlessly. Due to their backward looking and non-progressive politics, they play the sordid role of "godfatherism" and the status quo remains unchanged. Asking the right questions would have easily convinced any right thinking youth that the 'Not Too Young To Run' bill was merely a "Greek gift" or "booby trap" aimed at submerging the youths in the ocean of debt and poverty, while the septuagenarian politicians and their cohorts have their way.

In a country where the rate of unemployment is permanently on the increase, where most workers live from hand to mouth and many of our youths have no direction in life but wallow in self-delusion, we should really ask what they really mean with the phrase, "Not Too Young To Run?" Were they insinuating we are to run their dirty errands or we are not too young to run to save our nation from them? I believe they intended the former, even though they pretended they wanted the latter!

Wrestling power from the "Power that be" in this nation requires resolute determination by the youths who are adequately prepared to offer something better than what we have at the moment. Good intention alone won't conquer the structure of greed, selfishness, and self-centeredness that the current system has built in the hearts of many.

It is evidently clear that the people that need to be saved cannot see the danger they are living in. By and large, our generation needs to take proactive measures to save this nation urgently from this dangerously free-fall journey to disaster and perdition before it is too late.

With my experience, I have come to the practical realization that for the youths to achieve success in the public sphere and take over the steering wheel of leadership in the nation, they have to possess three important valuables, namely: idea; network; and money. Let me say, albeit unfortunately, that many of us only concentrate on money, while other necessary imperatives suffer gross neglect. I am not trying to say money is less important, it is equally important, but that should be after the other two have been put in place.

Money in itself is not power, but the proper utilization of money brings power. With a concrete idea and strong network, money will flow in naturally. An idea is a meticulously scrutinized intention, which has stood the test of time and can be trusted to be implementable. It forms the basis for ideology, with which one can operate life and manage situation. It must be carefully tied to sound morals, which will serve as a guiding light to illuminate the path of its operation and delineate every appearance of depravity.

Any idea that has no sound moral backing is certainly going to be counter-productive to its good intention. Many youths gallivant around today with many acclaimed good intentions, but what they have failed to do is connect it to a moral standard that can stand the test of time.

It is also dangerous for our youths to solely premise their intention on unfounded theoretical principles. Principles that are not practicable are as good as nothing. We have seen and read of many youths who ventured into communal politics with good intentions, having well-crafted and convincing manifestos, but at the end of the day, they delivered nothing close to their proposed desired objectives. To a large extent many of them have become problems that need emergency solution.

When my candidacy was revealed, many thought I was like others who would compromise at the middle of the sea, or that when the matter would become heated up and unbearable that I would negotiate a selfish landing platform at the shore. But little did they realize then that the lofty ideas I brought would translate into enormous passion that would drive my life as it is now.

My passion, defined, breaks forth in the following tributaries: Passion for good governance; passion for the helpless people; passion for doing the right thing, even when it hurts; passion for careful planning to make my lofty ideas become a reality; passion for sacrifice and selfless service toward nation building that calls for nothing but the complete liberation of the youths from the octopal clutches of poverty, ignorance, depravity, as well as to ensure the complete political emancipation of my people.

Compromising those passions, to me, would literally translate to cutting off my pulmonary artery. Such passion can only come as a result of morally sound ideologies that have been internalized over time.

In his book, *Think and Grow Rich*, Napoleon Hill highlighted the place of burning desire in the principle of success. He told the story of a man, Edwin C. Barnes, whose burning desire to form a business partnership with Thomas Edison led him to great riches. Just like many of the youths, Barnes started out with nothing significant; he had no money, little education and no influence, but he understood the fact that seizing a strategic opportunity to build up a network with the right person is a sure way to success.

Barnes presented himself to Mr. Edison at his laboratory and announced his only intention unequivocally. He wanted to go into partnership with Thomas Edison. Barnes did not get his partnership with Edison on his first interview. However he did get a chance to work in Edison's offices, at a very nominal wage, doing work that was unimportant to Edison, but most important to Barnes, because it gave him an opportunity to display his "merchandise" where his intended "partner" could see it.

The young man had a strong will to start from where he was with what he had. He knew the value of relationship with the right person.

He was ready to translate his desire into action by submitting himself to the power that could transform him. Many people lack that initiative. They want their tomorrow today and remain uncompromised.

Building a successful network means one has to first serve passionately. I am not talking about the superficial act of service or sycophantic gesture that many make today. I mean an intense desire to bring oneself low enough to learn from the people that are already upon the rungs of the ladder of success.

Even when Mr. Barnes had a single purpose at heart, which was quite different from what he was offered at his first interview with Thomas Edison, he served diligently by building trust, capacity and acquiring the necessary knowledge to achieve his intentions. Months went by, and apparently nothing happened to bring the coveted goal which Barnes had set up in his mind as his definite major purpose to pass. But something important was happening in Barnes' mind. He was constantly intensifying his desire to become a business associate to Edison.

The combination of Barnes relationship with Thomas Edison and the passionate desire with which he held his purpose at heart became the primary instrument that later brought him success. Mr. Edison had just perfected a new office device, known, at that time, as the Edison Dictating Machine (now the Ediphone). His salesmen were not enthusiastic over the machine. They did not believe it could be sold without great effort.

Barnes saw his opportunity. It had crawled in quietly, hidden in a queer looking machine which interested no one but Barnes and the inventor. Barnes knew he could sell the Edison Dictating Machine. He suggested this to Edison, and promptly got his chance. He did sell the machine. In fact, he sold it so successfully that Edison gave him a contract to distribute and market it all over the nation. Out of that, the business association grew the slogan, "Made by Edison and installed by Barnes." Out of it, Barnes had made himself rich in money. The network that Barnes built with Thomas served as a means to an end, money.

For the electioneering process, I spent over eleven million Naira without borrowing and I had no godfather. Money would have posed a major threat to my candidacy if all I focused on was cash inflow. Where could I have raised such amount without borrowing? It is also worth noting that all the funds did not come automatically. They came as an end to a means I had committed to since I was young. I have, over the years, built a strong network relationship with people, whose ideas aligned with mine; and I have jealously maintained and cherished those networks, relationships, hoping they would someday pay off.

Overtime, before I gained admission into the University, I had always looked up to people above me. I often gave a hand of help to the supposed middle-class people in my locality. I often collected their bags, ran errands for them, without any expectation for immediate reward. I did it solely to pave way for a lasting relationship. I sometimes washed their cars, and did for them other chores. Trust is one of the necessary virtues to build relationships. I never compromised my trustworthiness.

My musical skills and public performances were also instrumental to building my relationships' network.

By virtue of singing from one event to another, I met many prominent people. We exchanged contacts and complimentary cards. I took up the responsibility of nurturing and maintaining such relationships by keeping an open end conversation, finding mutual interest to connect; and I often sent nuggets to those people to keep them updated on my passion and ideologies.

Through some of our musical performances, I met the likes of Comrade Joseph Evah, Dr. Chris Ekiyor and Kingsley kuku who were of immense help during the election. Comrade Joseph Evah made branded T-shirts for the campaign. Kingsley Kuku was the man who later took us to perform at a symposium at Eko Hotel that was graced by His Excellency, Dr. Goodluck Ebele Jonathan. Our performance was electrifying.

Having this chain of network relationships, I maintained it through my social media platforms by consistently sharing with them my ideologies on leadership and success in life. Frequently leaving a trace of myself through text messages, I keep connecting with them through every available medium. That is the way to keep afloat in the system. Staying relevant means there must be some people above you that can give you a pull upward. I never let such people out of my network once I met them.

One thing is to have a network relationship, another thing is to give it life and dynamics by keeping it active. The network relationship must align with what you have. Connecting to the network relationship is simply gaining the ability to judiciously utilize the network. One must identify a mutual point of interest and propose a positive synergy that thrives on such mutual interest. A memory that quickly comes to mind was when we were trying to organize the Economic Summit for First Massive Literati in November, 2017.

Mr. Ken Etete is a man passionately interested in youths' inclusiveness in government. He was of tremendous help in making the summit a reality. Additionally, when the issue of my candidacy was raised, he was one of the reinforced shoulders upon which I stood.  He supported me massively during the election and still helped to secure my job when I didn't win the election. He called after the election; and we spoke extensively on the election.

He pointed out how successful I have become and encouraged me to push harder. I kept wondering why this man has an empowering interest in me.  He often refers to me as "Irrepressible James." He loves the passion I have developed over time for Nigeria and stated that we truly need creative leaders in Nigeria. We need creative leaders that can penetrate the powers and change the *status quo.* Nigeria will not fail if we have leaders that do not shy away from their responsibilities.

We need people who are creative and proactive toward bringing about solutions to the problems of the masses of our country. For me, helping the masses does not end at the polls.  In fact, my pro-masses work truly has just started. I have decided to embark on community projects in all the Local Government Areas in Ondo South senatorial district.

They lack most basic amenities that I have decided to assist to provide.

Many communities lack potable water, electricity, educational institutions with good buildings and educational facilities, among others. I believe solving the crucial and fundamental problems of the people will be a good way to make them feel the impact of a leader, irrespective of his or her political status.

I call it Corporate Social Responsibility or Personal Social Responsibility. You don't have to be in an elective political position before you can help others. By finding a societal problem and proffering appropriate solution, we can all become a leader in our precinct and initiate effective change in the lives of many. We should all keep in mind that the quality of our lives after we are gone from this world will be measured by our impact in the lives of others.

According to the teaching of Jesus Christ, He said if you helped one of these men, you have helped me. At every point, there is a need to connect to the needy around us and the fulfilment that comes with it is pleasurable and satisfying. The heart of every living being you have touched will always remember you until the end of time.

Whenever I think differently about this matter, the words of Job in the Bible always drive my mind back to the very fundamental reason of human existence. In the fourteenth chapter of the book of Job, the first two verses describe mortals, born of woman, as of few days and full of trouble: "They spring up like flowers and wither away; like fleeting shadows, they do not endure." (NIV). This brings expressly to mind my humble beginning and how I weathered through the stormy seas of life to get to where I am today.

All mortals have their own fair share of troubles in life; none of us have it all working perfectly at all times. But the beauty of humanity lies in our ability to offer a hand of help to each other, mutual encouragement and inspiration to encourage and fortify us against the storms of life.

In my stormy moment, most of the stories which I have told in this book, I did receive help from innumerable number of people who have ever since become endeared to my heart. I believe I also own humanity that much, to offer hope to the hopeless and give to as many people as I can, the will to live.

Like the fleeting shadow, the life of man is temporary. Only the good that one does during the few years is all that will count and outlive one. Every other pursuit is perishable. I wonder who has remembered the face, feelings and riches of men who lived one thousand years ago. They are all gone without a trace. Only those of them that left their footprints on the sands of time are remembered today.

Someday, I'll also share the same fate with them, my face and feelings will disappear in time and space. All my goals and dreams will efface, but that which will live on, I have committed to do, and that I will do till my last breath.

I wrote this book with one intention in mind: to hold the flag of hope flying high and to encourage everyone that will look at that flag that where there's a will, there must be a way. I am pragmatic and a realist. I strongly believe the goodness or evilness of our world is a reflection of our actions and decisions. If we begin to act right and make a good decision, our world will take the same turn. I am optimistic about Nigeria, and I am seriously convinced that providence has equipped us with every resource to make our nation better. What we are now experiencing is a direct and indirect consequences of our past actions and decisions. If we will sincerely pray and act the second stanza of our national anthem with heavens guiding our leaders right and helping our youths to know the truth, then it is a matter of when, and not if, for Nigeria shall certainly be great.

For the youths, the ball is in our court and we are at a critical crossroads of history. We are currently crucifying the geriatrics for what they have done and what they haven't, the wheel is already turning in our direction. We are the people of the moment, the strength of the nation. Our actions, inactions and decisions will be the history of tomorrow, and posterity will sit in judgment over our conduct.

Let me conclude this by one of the Lamentations of Prophet Jeremiah, Lamentations 3: 27, "It is good for a man to bear the yoke while he is young." While we still have the strength and valour, let us lift our nation high politically, economically and socially, that we may achieve fast economic development for the good of our people.

# CHAPTER SEVEN

# THE HEART OF THE MATTER

Life is a journey in many phases. We get born, we grow, we get involved in the activities of life, actively or passively, we age and transit. Within these phases, conditions and opportunities and challenges would definitely vary from one individual to another, community to community, even for nations; from one to another. Great concern it is that you and I discover the need to be actively engaged in the affairs of our domains, communities and nations, regarding how such places evolve in governance and relevant administration toward an all-encompassing purpose of bettering the lot of the lives circumscribed therein.

The ashes of your birth are not sufficient to hold you back from participating prosperously in how your community is managed and administered: for I was born poor but I rose above poverty to engage the senatorial platform of governance as a candidate canvassing and campaigning across multifarious terrains of extreme inconveniences.

The discouragement of your environment, talking about the pervasive indifference of so many older figures in the land who have given up on the possibilities of positive change; not withstanding, you must, as a youth, go beyond the reproach of the living-dead( the indifferent) and practically change the equation of squalor in the  midst of plenty; change the shameful grips of avarice and greed in the midst of abundance, evident across this nation through the change of the handlers of governance, as you bring it back to the virile and able youths. I was awashed with discouragement, yet I soared into participatory governance through electioneering involvement and pressure group administration alongside my contemporaries in FML.

Threats of death are not invincible in the face of the grace of the Living Creator to want to have you taken aback from communal contributions; and to want to have you write  off yourself from putting your hands on the plows of nation building: for, twice, death wrote me off but Grace restored me. How dare I waste the grace? Who knows whether I was born for such a time like this: a time to have the youths take over the reins of leadership and political governance of this great nation, part of whom you are as youths?

Some of you would want to excuse yourselves away from being involved in how you are governed, even from belonging to the category of the governors on the flimsiness of suffering in your present state and situation. You tell me: who do you know who contributed to humanity significantly without a taste of certain suffering? Even the Saviour of the world, according to the Holy Writ, suffered. I am told that, as flesh and blood, he learnt obedience through the things He suffered. Suffering is an integral part of living on Earth. It has its virtues. It helps you to develop empathy. Empathy makes you useful to others, and bursts the bubble of arrogance. I suffered hunger, neglect, financial inadequacies, and ill-health. Even in the hands of Talibanistic fake clergies, I suffered untold hardship. But, here we are, God- through you- is giving me a sense of purpose, part of today which you are, unto effective and effectual governance and administration of our Land, Nigeria, as we spread with great wings of the eagle, in our respective domains, flying in service to God, serving humanity selflessly. So, rise up!

Some of you have been bound and colonized within your minds to be second rated and to keep thinking that governance and rulership over resources and people, belong to some special individuals. The slavery mentality, amidst your brethren, has eaten your marrows. But this is a lie from the devil. Slavery is not the thinking and mind-set of the Creator concerning you. Stop being be-witched and hounded by the superstition of inferiority complex, inflicted upon your progenitor and which got passed over to you through their hereditary storytelling and body language of servitude. Break loose from it today!  Join me; join us to serve our communities, our people and our nation.

The way to go is forward. To forward- move is to start from where you are; yielding yourself to selfless service, from little tasks to major tasks. Wherever you find yourself, building strength, building capacity, and building your network relationships for increased personal net worth, without greed and avarice, not even the temptation of popularity at the expense of your colleagues, should dare wedge you on the journey.

May I, therefore, request that you secure a foundation in the immutable God, who has sent you here for a purpose, which includes the exercise of a peculiar leadership in your area of strength with the aim of using same as a tool to contribute to governance- your dominion mandate. So, you must find a solid spiritual base, howbeit in the true God, lest some spiritual marabout and vagabond cut you short.

Additional to the above is, I reiterate, the need for you to develop some competency and capability in all fronts: financially, scientifically, religiously and politically with local spice and universal infusion. Be the Jack of all trades but the master of all. Above all, be addicted to quality and selfless service rendition- make it a lifestyle. Then go ahead and present yourselves for elective office with a good and deliverable Manifesto that is designed to rescue our people from the current political parasites.

Let us do this together, changing our strategy from transactional politics to transformational politics, with a view to changing our nation and our world for good, with evident wellbeing and wellness of all. God bless.

# QUOTES

The Competent Youth is irrepressible. They are enlightened and aware of their environment. They criticize by taking constructive action to create the change they desire and believe in.

**Ken Etete**

---

The Competent Youth is the one Youth that knows
1. The necessary skills about a subject matter
2. Performs satisfactorily any related task that is relevant to the role.
3. Has a constant awareness of the limit of Competence in the area.

**Akpo Kentebe**

---

A competent Youth is one who has pruned himself to fit into the present day economy yet stays relevant even in the uncertain future.

**Ekoh Gene Ovabor**

---

The Competent Youth does not wait for time but seizes the opportunity to make an impact on society, realizing that time to make such an impact is short and indeed time waits for no one. Think of the founding founders of Nigeria. They took the bull by the horn and clamored for independence. The nation was governed by the Youth at independence. Any seemingly elderly individual was youthful at heart. He was vibrant and forward looking; wishing for a greater and prosperous Nigeria. This a Competent Youth. A Competent Youth is not one that sits on the fence but actively participates in societal activities-politics, sports, education, elections, etc. -to shape his and the destiny of his unborn children and generation. Staying by the corner and criticizing those at the helm of

affairs without any dedicated and active willingness to participate is gross incompetence. Participation doesn't mean actively vying for a position or office but means supporting an ideal and a course that seeks a greater nation ultimately.
**Dr. Preye Angaye**

---

Millennial all over the world are clamouring for power without sitting down to understand what it actually means. Power of any kind can kill, it can also make alive, it gives hope and also dashes hope. When you want power, you must truly ask yourself what you want power for. Being a Competent Youth in this generation means you understand the intrigue dynamics, responsibilities and demands of power and you are willing to deplore power positively. The Competent Youth is a youth with the needed capacity, relevant knowledge and ability to turn promises to performances, hopes to realities and bills to law. This is a must read for all millenials...
**Michael Ogunsina**

---

A Competent Youth is the youth that knows his right from left knowing when to speak and when to act; being selfless in approach to matters and most importantly, knowing when to take the bull by the horns.
**Michael Useghan**

---

A Competent Youth is the individual who is ambitious enthusiastic, energetic and promising. He/she knows the expectation of the family and the community the individual belongs to as the future leader. It is the individual who wants to deliver at the right time. He sets a goal and works towards achieving the goal no matter the challenges because he believes there are opportunities in every challenges.
**Mrs. Wemimo Akinduro**

A Competent Youth is not only one who has foresight, creative and innovative with developmental objectives for community, society and the country, but is also well grounded in ethics, morales, integrity and probity, sufficient enough to resist greed for money and is not corrupt and can not sell his/her conscience for power, position or money and would not be tribal or nepotistic in all ramifications of life's dealings.
**Mr. Stephen Obubo**

---

Competent Youth means not withstanding whatsoever odds against you as a youth you must believe you have necessary ability or skills to do something well or well enough to meet a standard.
**Ajama Timothy Emmanuel**

---

A Competent Youth is a young person who is always ready and willing to make things happen and work out for the betterment of his welfare and of others against all odds using the acronym called VASK(Value, Attitute, Skill and Knowledge) to work this out.
**Ehi Samson Light**

---

A Competent Youth is a young adult who is ready to achieve his desire goal for the improvement of his society, irrespective of the challenges (socio-political, enviromental or economic factors) that comes his way.
**Prince Opeyemi Omisore**

---

The Competent Youth "who are they"? The nation awaits the earnest manifestation of the Joshua Generation... a generation imbued with knowledge, understanding and wisdom. A generation imbibed with unconditional patriotism. A generation with the capacity to lift a nation and direct her path away from meandering in the wilderness of

nothingness. Those are the competent youth the world awaits and the nation desires.
**George Ashiru**

---

A young person who dares to do, and to do effectively, what elders have made a mess of. Example: Fixing Nigeria.
**Edikan Macauley**

---

A Competent Youth is a volunteer who accepts the cooperate social responsibilities of the community, he finds himself regardless of all odds just to make the society an egalitarian one for everybody.
**Yunusa Yakubu Itumeyi**

---

A Competent Youth is one who act with PASSION that leads to ACTIONS, PERSISTENT in prospering and having a POSITIVE mental capacity to bring RESULTS.
**Igbang Joe Ugo**

---

A Competent Youth is a that fellow who is vibrant...energetic...goalgetter...risk bearer who is ready to be up to the task in every situation and making an impact as an individual to the society at large.
**Omowunmi Sodunke**

---

Competent Youth is a youth that is ready to sacrifice, take risk and participate in leadership of a community, state or country that will lead to transformation of the people.
**Ariaye Ijokumoh Richard**

---

When one person is competent, they can devote what they know to do a definite task or come in handy to circumstances and they are capable to transfer this ability between different situations.
**Namu Micah**